AARON TRIVETT

THE PREPPER'S SURVIVAL BIBLE

10 BOOKS IN 1

Protect Your Family During Natural Disasters and Societal Collapse. Learn to Be Self-Sufficient Without Depending on Others Anymore.

THE PREPPER'S SURVIVAL GUIDE

10 BOOKS IN 1:

PROTECT YOUR FAMILY DURING NATURAL DISASTERS AND SOCIETAL COLLAPSE.

LEARN TO BE SELF-SUFFICIENT WITHOUT DEPENDING ON OTHERS ANYMORE.

Aaron Trivett

© Copyright 2022 by Aaron Trivett - All rights reserved.

The following Book is reproduced below with the goal of providing information that is as accurate and reliable as possible. Regardless, purchasing this Book can be seen as consent to the fact that both the publisher and the author of this book are in no way experts on the topics discussed within and that any recommendations or suggestions that are made herein are for entertainment purposes only. Professionals should be consulted as needed prior to undertaking any of the action endorsed herein.

This declaration is deemed fair and valid by both the American Bar Association and the Committee of Publishers Association and is legally binding throughout the United States.

Furthermore, the transmission, duplication, or reproduction of any of the following work including specific information will be considered an illegal act irrespective of if it is done electronically or in print. This extends to creating a secondary or tertiary copy of the work or a recorded copy and is only allowed with the express written consent from the Publisher. All additional right reserved.

The information in the following pages is broadly considered a truthful and accurate account of facts and as such, any inattention, use, or misuse of the information in question by the reader will render any resulting actions solely under their purview. There are no scenarios in which the publisher or the original author of this work can be in any fashion deemed liable for any hardship or damages that may befall them after undertaking the information described herein.

Additionally, the information in the following pages is intended only for informational purposes and should thus be thought of as universal. As befitting its nature, it is presented without assurance regarding its prolonged validity or interim quality. Trademarks mentioned are done without written consent and can in no way be considered an endorsement from the trademark holder

INTRODUCTION 7

PART 1: LEARNING FROM HISTORY TO PREVENT FUTURE DEJÀ VU 18

    "Natural" disasters 19

    Anthropogenic and social phenomena 20

    "Technological" catastrophes 21

    The acceleration of the Anthropocene 23

    The "health" catastrophes 24

    Historiographical myopia 25

    Breaking events 26

    The role of the state 27

    The media system 29

    Memory 31

PART 2: WATER 33

    Right tools, the right know-how 37

    Water sources 43

    Water purification 44

    Water filtration 44

PART 3: FOOD AND HOW TO STORE IT 45

    The rule of three 47

    Step one: a survival mindset 52

    Begin food planning 55

    Pressure canning 58

    Water Bath Canning 62

    Water Bath canning explained step by step 65

    Steps for preparing and sterilizing canning jars: 65

    Frequently asked questions 68

    Food supplies for evacuation 69

PART 4: THE PREPPER'S HOME DEFENSE 71

    Surviving the elements 78

    Miscellaneous preparations 86

    The BOB (Bug-Out-Bag) checklist 89

Basement shelters 96
Public shelters 97
Self-defense and weapons 97
Self-injury vs. self-defense 98
Survival knives 99
Decide what kind of shelter to build or use 100

PART 5: OFF-GRID LIVING 104

How to build a photovoltaic panel 107
How to properly start a fire 110
How to navigate 114

PART 6: HYGIENE 120

PART 7: FIRST AID AND NATURAL MEDICINE 126

First aid kit 126
First aid and medicines: keep healthy 127
Medical kits and containers 128
Medicines and drugs 128
Customization 129
Natural medicines 134

PART 8: KNOT TYING GUIDE 139

Stopping knots 139
Origins 140
Strengths and weaknesses 140
Applications 140
Junction knots 140
Sheet knot or flag 142
Strengths and weaknesses 142
Applications 142
Eye knots 142
Gassa D'Amante 143
Strengths and weaknesses 143
Applications 143
Scorsoi knots 143

    Strengths and weaknesses 143
    Origins 144
    Knots 144
    Strengths and weaknesses 144
    Winding knots 144
    Utility applications and bindings 145

PART 9: THE IMPORTANCE OF THE COMMUNITY 146

PART 10: THE PREPPER'S COOKBOOK 149

CONCLUSION 201

EMERGENCIES 202

ESSENTIAL ITEMS CHECKLIST 203

ACKNOWLEDGEMENTS 206

REFERENCES 207

INTRODUCTION

Modern convenience offers our society much more than previous generations could have wished for or considered. However, our ancestors had some critical things that are rare nowadays. The skills and attitude they needed to overcome daily challenges seem to be things that most have just missed out on.

Life is more manageable now. However, I have come to wonder how all modern conveniences offer the principles of self-sufficiency were passed in exchange for a trade-off. It seems that many people today do not even have the basic skills that would become necessary to ensure personal safety and survival in an emergency.

I hope this book can lead to the recognition that the hard work and virtues of self-reliance exercised generations ago are as important today as they have always been.

Disasters frequently happen, whether isolated situations or significant news events and everyone should take note. Spending time reflecting, learning new skills, and assembling the proper equipment could help if an emergency touches your family.

It is about developing the right mindset and approaching life from a position of vigilance. It is about keeping one step ahead of our many risk factors. Today is the best time to start. It is too late to entertain that first thought about survival when a real threat is knocking at the front door.

The potential for devastation is not a pleasant subject to think about. It is not hard to see how many people have become accustomed to complacent attitudes. It is an extraordinary time marked by new and incredible tools. Most people access 118 emergency services directly from their pocket by cell phone. Those same phones can often send e-mail, and text messages, surf the Internet, and retrieve the latest news and weather reports.

Many people can push a button in their cars and quickly call an ambulance at the first sign of trouble.

It is a double-edged sword. So, a lot of people today have false senses of security reinforced by all their conveniences. Many derive great and undue comfort knowing their credit cards are at hand. However, phones or the paper and plastic in our wallets would not be foolproof in the midst of disaster or its aftermath. Like the men and women of a generation or two earlier, we still genuinely need the know-how and ingenuity to rely on ourselves alone in the event of difficult situations that require it.

Today, most would rather not worry about what is broken. It's a disposable company where people expect their staff to work, tossing it aside at the first sign of trouble. If the item is essential enough, they will send it for repair. My father bought something new when the situation called for it, but he never put the old one in the trash. After all, that old part was still good for spare parts. He would not call someone else to fix his problems because he knew he could just as quickly do it himself.

After an emergency, you may very well find that there is no person available to answer the phone. Too few today are willing to devote even a fraction of time or effort to achieve their solutions. Usually, all it takes is a phone call and some money to pass that work on to someone else.

It is fantastic that such a dramatic change in skills and attitudes has occurred in such a short period. Many people in this modern era would be lost without the ability to lean on another. It is a bit frightening that so many are so far removed from the spirit exhibited by my father's generation.

It is said that "ignorance is bliss," and I think it best describes the approach most people take toward preparedness. Survival planning is fundamental because of an extension of that earlier ethic. It's about accounting for risks, considering needs, and having contingencies on hand should the time come when you can depend only on yourself, your friends, and your family.

Many people would rather not entertain the thought of a survival situation, and I feel that some people see preparedness as a practice of pessimism.

I certainly would not consider myself among those who see the glass as half-empty; on the contrary. I have always been a problem solver, which has laid the foundation for all my efforts. I have long had a unique ability to identify problems and, more importantly, to find workable solutions.

Comfort and even survival in the wake of a disaster can depend on the solutions you put together well in advance. Preparing for the worst and expecting it are two very different mindsets. I don't look over my shoulder, hoping to find trouble, but I know I would be ready if the problem were to see me.

It would help if you did not lose sight of the fact that trouble is out there. My extensive travels and first-hand glimpses in the aftermath of some of the world's most devastating natural disasters have only strengthened my convictions about the value of proper planning. Everyday calm efforts are the only way to ensure that the basics of survival-namely shelter, water, and food-are ready and quickly available when disaster introduces chaos into a community.

It is easier for many to consider disaster impersonally and from a distance. It would help if you took time to imagine yourself and your family directly in the shoes of those wondering what they will do after a disaster has taken everything. Families who survive destructive tornadoes or violent earthquakes, for example, face the loss of their homes and often the reality that their precious possessions are lost forever.

Wildfires spread each year rapidly through forested areas in many areas. Families in affected areas often receive no more than an hour's notice when it is time to evacuate. It is hard to imagine having such a narrow window to run through the house, deciding what to take and what pieces of a hard-earned livelihood the family should let go to ruin.

In a typical and even destructive house fire, many families will return and find some degree of hope in the form of salvageable items. They may pick up some family heirlooms or some furniture from the rubble.

You should not take your life or part of your prosperity for granted. I have looked into the eyes of those who have survived the catastrophic loss. Stunned and confused would be the best description I can offer for the expressions on faces when people realize they have just lost everything.

You cannot stop disaster, but you can do your best to mitigate the level of damage it brings. Preparedness is a way of life that recognizes that bad things happen. It is a quest to develop the flexibility to deal with unforeseen challenges.

Life is a wild and fantastic journey, and experiences along the way have continually led to a more explicit focus on a critical nugget of truth. A well-lived life is about anticipating problems, facing challenges when they arise, and becoming more muscular on the other side. The further ahead you can set your goals, the better off you will be.

Preparation is empowerment. There is a particular strength that comes from knowing that while a disaster would test your emotions, you could cope, live safely and ensure the well-being of your family. Well-prepared people are also able to provide a certain level of comfort.

Consider this book as a road map to some peace of mind and take the first steps along that path.

Disasters have been and always will be a regular part of life on this planet. Floods, tornadoes, hurricanes, or fires that harm people across the country or the world could quickly break your neighborhood as they will tomorrow. It is a roll of the dice to ignore the dangers.

Preparation begins quickly enough with excellent and honest thinking. A minimum plan should at least take into account the basics of survival. Without food, water, and adequate shelter, you would not make it long.

Those unfamiliar with preparedness planning should apply those needs to the real-life possibilities from where and how your families live. It is at that point that you can begin to forge some solutions.

Regardless of where you live, it is about breaking down and solving the many small challenges that any disaster and its aftermath might present to your family. A diligent prepper will have the appropriate equipment if an emergency requires a quick escape. The well-prepared will have sufficient first aid knowledge to immediately assist the injured should a disaster slow down paramedic response time.

It is not only a matter of developing plans but also of working with them. Families should practice, familiarize and develop comfort in the solutions devised for each reasonable risk. It is an ongoing process. It involves keeping the mind focused on safety. The first natural step is to overcome a dangerous notion held by too many. No one should think, "This will never happen to me."

That is the reality. Disasters change lives. Those who harbor excessive confidence in modern improvements are setting themselves up for rude awakenings should they find themselves in the path of nature's forces.

As some are too comfortable in their technologies, others place too much trust in an admittedly robust emergency warning infrastructure. Everyone is fortunate to live in an age when warning of potentially dangerous situations has never been better. In addition to traditional airborne sirens, people have instant news alerts, occasional television substitutions, and autodialed telephone messages. The above disasters demonstrate that warning alone is not enough to ensure safety.

Preparation can provide some assurance. You would know that there is enough to eat and a means to stay warm and dry. The idea of acting today for the sake of tomorrow is not a new concept.

It is somewhat puzzling why survival preparedness is so foreign to many when most prepare for life's significant risks in other ways. Every driver requires auto insurance with complete confidence that they will arrive at every destination without a scratch or dent.

Survival preparation is a form of insurance that requires more thought and commitment. It is not as simple as writing a check, although it considers the most critical issues in life: the people you love and the skin you are in. In this regard, most people are pretty good at preparation when it comes to taking care of their things.

Indeed, people can overcome devastating circumstances without having the proper contingencies. The question is whether you agree with the prospect of suffering more than necessary. The unprepared may have it more accessible, whether it is an earthquake or a three-day power outage. It is simply a matter of developing the proper knowledge and conserving some supplies. It is merely a matter of common sense.

Preparedness is often portrayed in the media through the eyes of those who are convinced that government collapse, mass terrorism, or some other world-changing event is coming. Some may feel that survival planning is the pursuit of those who worry too much. That is easy to understand.

Preparation is not about judgment day. It is about every day. It is about the neighborhood reorganizing after the heavy storm and the township faltering after the earthquake. Across the country, people will find themselves in untenable positions every day of the week.

Readiness offers a better approach to life. After assembling the proper tools and supplies, you can put worries aside and feel good about where your family is. Certain ease comes from knowledge; thinking ahead and knowing your family is a step forward of anything Mother Nature can bring. Planning, thinking, and building a stockpile of supplies is simply a matter of planning. From there, you could comfortably hope never to have to harvest your efforts.

If you haven't thought about it yet, here are the top ten must-have items for a viable survival kit. No fancy technology: it's down to business here.

10. Fire starter kit

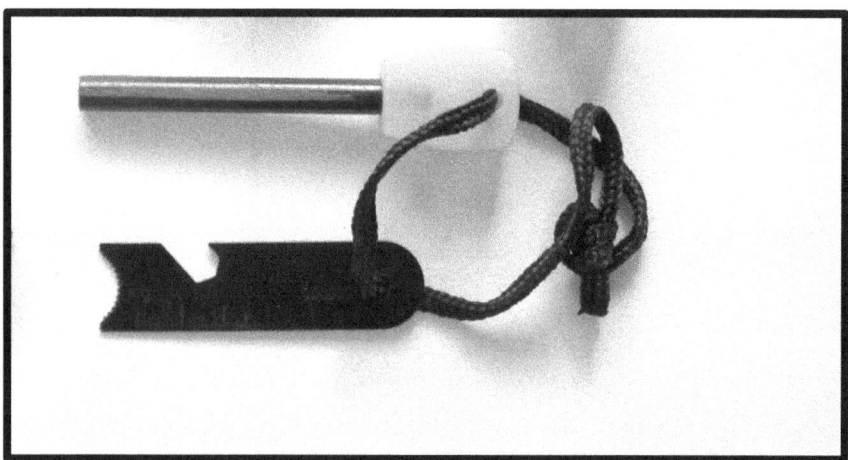

Essential to a good kit, the magnesium tinder is the flint of our time. Scouts, at least once in their lives, have experienced it. Most good ones allow about 12,000 ignitions.

9. Rope

It can be used for many things and is never enough, so equip yourself with a reasonably substantial skein: better to always abound.

8. Suture needle

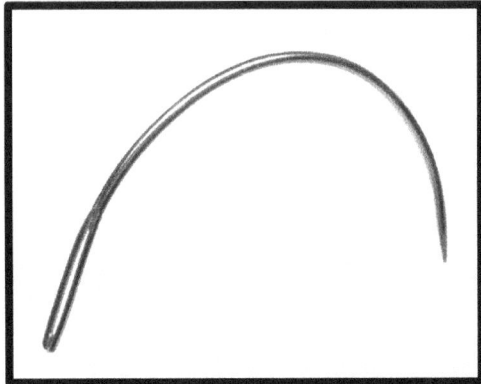
Credit Photo: Pavel Krok - Own work

Essential in emergencies (in the most desperate situations, it can be at the "good," naturally-substituted for a regular sewing needle), the suture needle requires skill in its use. But in a pinch, survival instincts prevail, and while not a doctor or nurse, a suture needle can always be a lifeline.

7. Safety pin

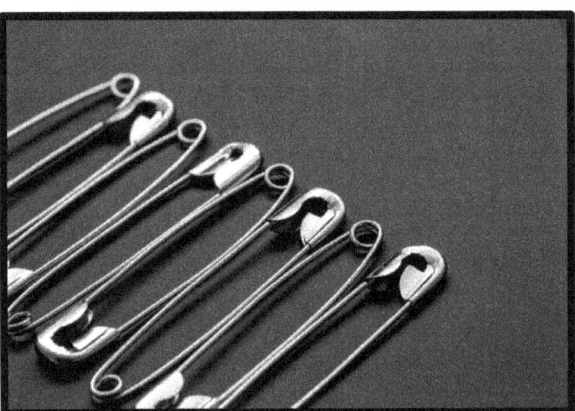

Timeless and unfailing, the safety pin (preferably more than one pair) is a multipurpose accessory. It can be adapted into a fish hook in pressing need, join fabrics or frank webbing of rigid materials, and pierce surfaces.
In addition, when sterilized in boiling water, it can turn into a medical needle. What more could you want?

6. Multipurpose accessories

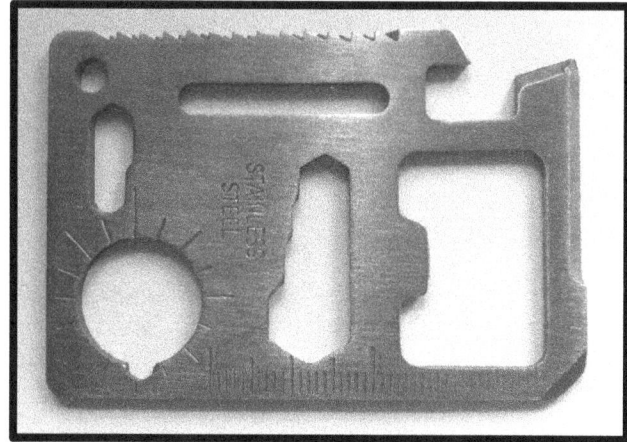

Useful in various circumstances, the multipurpose tool is an essential accessory. Ruler but also a screwdriver, awl, mini-knife, and more: this tool could be helpful to you for different purposes.

5. Sterile gauze

Useful for wounds and bleeding, but also other things. Gauze (preferably sterile) can be faithful allies in the most chaotic moments. For example, I was improvising a water filtration system. Or keep pesky insects away.

4. Whistle

Titanic taught it: a whistle is always a good companion. There are many models and shapes, but only one thing matters: it makes lots and lots of noise.

3. Compass

Moss is not enough: to juggle nature or catastrophic situations, you need more than that. A compass is essential. If millesimal (like military ones), even better, this compass also allows you to measure distances.

2. Survival knife

Ban over-accessorized utility knives: if you want to save your skin, it's a good idea to opt for a tool that performs its function to the fullest. Instead, add a few more small accessories to your kit, but don't compromise the operation of a good, sturdy, large blade with other small, semi-useless tools.

Water filter

Well, yes: if the human body is composed mainly of water, the first thing to think about to survive is precisely a water filter. The Swiss company "Lifestraw" holds the lead in making such devices.

These devices (those for individual users) allow drinking directly from the river or puddle under the circumstances, filtering impurities, metals, and viruses for up to 1,000 liters.

PART 1: LEARNING FROM HISTORY TO PREVENT FUTURE DEJÀ VU

When referring to history, the emergency/reconstruction binomial is usually associated in the first instance with major war events, that is, the upheavals they caused, their multiple repercussions, and the problematic attempts to restore normalcy. It is no coincidence that when faced with any major disaster, the parallelism clicks almost automatically, "It's like a war!"

If we circumscribe the reflection to the twentieth century, World War II, in particular, has taken on a paradigmatic value from this point of view, being interpreted-for various and well-founded reasons as the absolute most traumatic event in the global history of the twentieth century. For a century, that enshrined the primacy of politics over nature as the principal architect of catastrophic traumas for humanity.

However, the contemporary age-and, more generally, the entire history of humanity-has experienced countless other events or phenomena of extreme criticality, which, albeit on different geographical and temporal scales, have been perceived, faced, and experienced as actual emergencies.

Not only war, therefore, should be accorded the status of an emergency. Nor is it only the post-war periods that have required great works of reconstruction material but also political, economic, and moral of human societies. This observation appears even more evident during the current Covid-19 pandemic.

To deal with the theme of emergency/reconstruction from a historical perspective, we will not be dealing with wars nor other categories of tragic events, such as those arising from political uprisings and conflicts, terrorist or criminal acts, or the collapse of institutional or economic systems. These are all phenomena that have a clear and exclusive anthropogenic connotation.

First, while making no taxonomic claims, we will try to outline an overview, distinguishing between "natural," "technological," and "health" disasters, but also pointing out some intrinsic commonalities. We will consider other types of emergencies, which originate in the complexity, instability, and fragility of the relationship between humans and nature. We will then shift our attention to their historical relevance from the mid-20th century to the present, focusing on three crucial junctures: the debate between state and civil society, the role of the media system, and the importance of memory.

"Natural" disasters

The category of "natural" disasters includes disasters caused by various calamities such as earthquakes, volcanic eruptions, floods, etc... The main difference between such disasters from war emergencies, and the reason why they are called "natural," lies in their genesis, that is, the fact that they do not have strictly or solely artificial causes like wars. With all evidence, it is not the man who triggers a hurricane, volcanic explosion, or earth tremor. Nevertheless, several scholars have pointed out that putting the adjective "natural" in quotation marks is correct.

Although any extreme event is potentially devastating, it gives rise to catastrophes only in cases where it interacts with the human presence on the planet, causing casualties and extensive material damage. As British scientist, Karl Western wrote:

From a certain point of view, a disaster becomes a disaster only when humans or environments created by humans are involved. An avalanche in an uninhabited valley or an earthquake in the Arctic are geophysical events; they are not disasters.

In other words, the impact of cataclysms on the ecumene produces "natural" catastrophes. Any "natural" hazard is always linked to human social activity. And this interaction between destructive agents and human communities has at least two implications on the conceptual level.

Anthropogenic and social phenomena

In the first place, it is the degree of the devastation of the human settlements affected, rather than the power of the phenomenon as such, that determines the severity of the event (taking the case of earthquakes, it could be argued that the Mercalli scale is more relevant than the Richter scale). From this overtly anthropocentric perspective, the importance of a calamity is established by the material and demographic consequences on the human environment. At the same time, there is no direct proportionality relationship between the destructive agent's intrinsic force and the episode's dramatic nature.

For example, among the great earthquakes of our time, one of the most catastrophic was the 2010 earthquake in Port-au-Prince (Haiti), which, although not of an exceptional magnitude (7.0), caused at least 230,000 deaths (other estimates put the death toll at more than 300,000) and affected about 3 million people.

Conversely, the most powerful earthquake ever recorded by modern instrumentation happened in the 1960 Valdivia (Chile) earthquake, which reached a magnitude of 9.5- represents a less disastrous case (no more than 3,000 people were left under the rubble). Because it was located in an area with low population density and buildings constructed mainly of wood, a few years later, the 1964 Alaska earthquake (of magnitude 9.2) claimed only a few dozen lives, despite the enormous energy released.

That does not detract from the fact that these powerful seismic tremors had geophysical effects on a global scale, even going so far as to impart slight changes to the shape of the planet. But from an anthropocentric point of view, their impact was less devastating than other catastrophic phenomena.

Although one might object to the permissibility of rankings based on the number of deaths or material damage, the statistical fact remains and has its interest.

On the other hand, even highly violent earth tremors far from population centers. For example, an epicenter of an ocean that generated a giant tsunami can cause colossal catastrophes. That happened on December 26, 2004, with tsunamis that struck Southeast Asia's coasts and forced some 250,000 deaths, half a million injuries, and more than three million displaced people.

Second, "natural" disasters and catastrophes should also be interpreted as social phenomena. Not only because they involve profound upheavals in the organizational structure, daily dynamics, and affective and emotional fabric of affected societies, but also because the specific vulnerabilities of social systems shape them. The interaction between the type of destructive agent, the geo-historical environment, and the type of society shapes the forms of disaster.

That is, an earthquake or a flood can cause emergencies of different degrees according to variables that affect not only the geomorphological nature of the affected place. Also, population density, urban planning conditions, technological development, scientific knowledge, and, more generally, the social system formed over time.

In this sense, on the one hand, the disastrous impact of an extreme event is determined at least in part by the past evolution of the affected community. On the other hand, it produces medium- and long-term social effects. In short, the nexus with history is complex and two-way.

"Technological" catastrophes

The preceding remarks lead one to blur the conventional distinction between "natural" and "technological" (or "man-made," according to Anglo-Saxon terminology) disasters. This category refers to those disasters derived from human activities, or more precisely, dependent on the use of the various technologies developed by men, such as significant chemical, nuclear, or engineering accidents. In the history of the twentieth century, a paradigmatic case in point is the 1986 Chernobyl accident, with the failure that occurred at the Soviet nuclear power plant and the resulting environmental disaster that cost lives or caused tragic health problems for an unknown number of people and other living beings.

On closer inspection, examples of this type are far more numerous. They include all emergencies originating from human errors, inexperience, and imprudence: among the most frequent are the collapse of dams and the resulting floods. In their diversity, these are disasters that do not arise from the impact of external agents on human communities but rather as a consequence of risks taken, more or less consciously, in applying technical-scientific knowledge.

However, even in these cases, catastrophe arises from the interaction between various factors: the type of technology and the level of hazard, certainly, but also the environmental context, political decisions, social organization, economic resources, cultural legacies, and so on. In short, the complexity of connections between various elements of vulnerability is at the root of "technological" disasters and "natural" ones.

The dividing line between the one and the other turns out to be very blurred.

Not to mention that the two types of disasters sometimes appear in close correlation. Take the case of the Japanese city of Fukushima, home to a nuclear power plant that, in March 2011, was hit by an exceptional magnitude (9.0) earthquake, followed by a devastating tsunami with waves exceeding ten meters in height.

The combination of the two "natural" phenomena produced an impact far beyond the safety levels envisioned in the plant's design by blowing up three reactors' cooling systems and causing radioactivity release.

As Japan is a country at the forefront of earthquake-resistant construction and providing prevention, warning, and emergency response tools, the Fukushima "accident" did not have the catastrophic outcomes that would have been seen elsewhere. On the other hand, the nuclear disaster was still serious. Above all, it is the consequence not only of the combination of "natural" events and "technological" danger but also of the political choice to build a power plant in an area of very high seismic risk. Fukushima represents a perfect example, in short, of the complex interaction of factors that are at the origin of a baleful emergency.

The acceleration of the Anthropocene

The dichotomy between "natural" and "man-made" catastrophes seems even more inadequate if we introduce the notion of the Anthropocene into the reflection. As is well-known, the term was adopted in 2000 by the Dutch chemist Paul Crutzen (formerly Nobel Prize winner in 1995) to define a new period in Earth's history. Marked by the pressure of human activities on the planet's ecology and opened in the late eighteenth century with the inauguration of an energy regime based on fossil fuels.

From 2000 onward, Crutzen's theories have been followed by various other formulations. The concept has experienced increasing fortune, not only in the scientific literature: in recent years, some interest has been aroused, for example, by the Anthropocene Project, which through photographic exhibitions in several countries (including, in Italy, at the MAST in Bologna), popular publications and a documentary made in collaboration with photographer Edward Burtynsky, has illustrated to the general public some of the invasive effects of the irresponsible impact of human activities on the environment.

But while interpretations of the origins of the Anthropocene diverge, some even trace them back to the discovery of fire; the less controversial view is that human influence on the "Earth system" has grown dramatically since 1945, reaching levels that are now environmentally unsustainable. Soaring population, global urbanization, exponential increases in energy consumption, the accumulation of carbon dioxide in the atmosphere, and the worldwide invasion of plastic goods are just some of the dynamics that have imparted a "great acceleration" to man's impact on the planet since the mid-20th century.

This set of processes has had among its consequences the increase of a specific type of slow and silent disasters-and not as deflagrating as an earthquake-determined by the increasingly complex interaction between human activities and different ecosystems.

The most significant phenomenon is undoubtedly the climate emergency, which some intellectuals now consider irreversible. The warming of the atmosphere caused, mainly by a concentration of carbon dioxide that has grown more than eightfold since 1945, has increased the likelihood of devastating droughts and catastrophic precipitation.

Prominent examples include the Sahel (drought and famine) in the 1970s-1980s and the Bay of Bengal (cyclones and floods) in 1970 and 1991.

But as complex as it is to demonstrate the strict consequentiality of individual factors. For example, a direct relationship between certain human activities repeated over time, rising global temperatures, and desertification or flooding of a specific area of the world in the Anthropocene, environmental crises are increasingly severe, widespread, and frequent. And their increasing intensity reveals "the peculiarity of the contemporary age also in environmental terms."

The "health" catastrophes

The current Covid-19 pandemic has brought back to the forefront the "health" emergency that has been very frequent in human history, even in contemporary times. Without needing to recall the plague waves of earlier centuries, it is sufficient to recognize the various viral epidemics that have affected the 20th century: from the severe flu known as "Spanish flu," which killed tens of millions of people worldwide between 1918 and 1920, to the more recent cases of Avian Flu, AIDS, Ebola, Sars, and the "Coronavirus" of the present day.

These are all infectious diseases that originated through zoonosis. It is due to a species jump of a pathogenic element that, at some point in its evolution, manages to transfer from a given animal species to humans.

To which can be added a whole series of serious bacterial infections, such as the spread of typhoid or cholera (the last major cholera epidemic in Italy was in 1973).

The differences between these diseases and phenomena such as earthquakes or floods are pretty evident and concerning; first, the spatial-temporal dimension: having an epidemic, or pandemic, character, health emergencies affect large areas of the world over a more extended period.

The damage caused is also partially dissimilar since epidemics do not cause material destruction (at least not directly). And the problems affected societies face, both in the acute phase of the health crisis and in the recovery and returned to normalcy, are different. However, here again, the emergency underscores how human existence is intertwined with the biological environment, how humans are embedded in nature, and how human history is inseparable from that of the planet on which it takes place.

The advent of the Anthropocene has not broken the link. While it has meant a more extraordinary ability for humans to separate their productive activities from the rhythms of nature, it has not allowed effective enfranchisement from biological hazards. On the contrary, the alteration of eco-systemic balances has increased the risk of health crises, to some extent correlated with environmental devastation: "the destruction of ecosystems." Writes David Quammen, "seems to have among its consequences the increasingly frequent appearance of pathogens in larger areas than the original ones," thus increasing the likelihood that some viruses will come into contact with humans and be able to adapt to the new species.

Historiographical myopia

Different types of "non-war" emergencies have occurred throughout history, with increased frequency and severity in the era marked by the "great acceleration" of the Anthropocene. Nevertheless, historians of the contemporary age have shown only sporadic or fluctuating attention to such phenomena, which have often been neglected, if not excluded, from their horizons of inquiry.

Ecological crises and other major catastrophic events have rarely entered the historical narratives devoted to the twentieth century and at most have been confined to an autonomous field of research - environmental history - relegated to a defiladed position in the overall reconstructions of social, economic, and political processes. In one of her recent volumes, Gabriella Gribaudi identified the probable underlying reason for this gap: "'natural' disasters are considered accidents and therefore beyond human control or action, and thus their study is left entirely to the hard sciences.

In short, something similar has happened to what Indian writer Amitav Ghosh has found regarding the lack of presence of climate change and its effects on the themes of contemporary literature.

As if the latter has been affected by a form of "great blindness"-or "great alienation," to translate the book's original title, The Great Derangement"-to one of the significant problems of today's age. Here, if historiography has not been blind, at least it has been myopic and has struggled to focus on certain phenomena in the overall picture of the contemporary age.

Breaking events

The fact remains that, like wartime conflicts, other disasters can also have significant historical repercussions, not only because of their impact on demography and human habitat but also on the social fabric, the economy, and sometimes even politics.

These are phenomena that raise mortality rates far beyond ordinary levels and, in some cases-earthquakes and floods, in particular-destroy infrastructure, buildings, dwellings, assets, and objects of daily life. The social and economic consequences are profound, and they are often so even in the case of emergencies that do not produce material destruction, as in the case of environmental crises and pandemics. It is a kind of devastation that bears strong similarities to the damage caused by wars: consider, as the most glaring example, the aerial bombings of World War II.

Thus, these are phenomena that, although in different ways than war conflicts, can induce political changes: it is not uncommon for a disaster to be followed by a regime crisis, as was the case in Nicaragua after the December 1972 earthquake that destabilized the Somoza dictatorship; or even a situation of the geopolitical order, as in the Indian subcontinent, with the insurgency, civil war and subsequent proclamation of the independent state of Bangladesh provoked by the epochal 1970 flood in the Bay of Bengal.

Sometimes the caesura that the traumatic event imprints on a community's life are amplified by how political power conducts reconstruction. Several case studies offer a fascinating insight from this perspective, highlighting specific state systems' authoritarian and centralist character. As was the case in Tashkent, Uzbekistan, under the Soviet regime: here, after the 1966 earthquake, the city was rebuilt according to a cultural and urbanistic model entirely unrelated to the past, sacrificing what remained of the traditional neighborhoods, completely redesigning the topography, and imposing a new architectural and urbanistic style to create "the model city of Soviet modernity in the backward suburbs."

Elsewhere, too, and in very different historical settings, reconstruction projects have been implemented that have profoundly transformed the territory compared to the past. Such is the case of a town like Gibellina, Sicily, which moved miles away from the original settlement after the 1968 earthquake in the Belice Valley. Or of the reconstruction undertaken in the Indian state of Gujarat following the devastating earthquake of January 2001, conducted through mixed forms of financing-private and public, governmental and international-that pursued an urban rebuilding project far removed from the housing traditions of the ancient caste system, arousing no small amount of resistance among the local populations.

Disasters, then, imprint a periodizing rupture on different scales. First, they mark a caesura in the ordinary life of people and communities invested by the emergency, for whom the flow of time is divided into "a before" and "an after." The hope for a restoration of the previous "normality" is bound to remain unfulfilled. And the events often acquire the value of actual historical turning points, triggering significant changes in various spheres: from environmental policy to urban topography, from the cultural perception of risk to technological and economic development.

The theme, therefore, lends itself to investigation from multiple angles. We will now try - keeping in the background the history of republican Italy punctuated by a long sequence of disasters to introduce some insights into three leading agents in the unfolding of the emergency and restart: the state, the media, and memory.

The role of the state

Whether amid the emergency phase or in the transition to the reconstruction or restart phase, all types of disasters redefine the relationship between the public and private sectors, primarily assigning a crucial role to the state. In the face of an emergency, the public authorities and institutions have the task of ensuring relief and first aid, then managing the exit from the crisis and the return to the ordinary, and finally arranging solutions to avoid, as far as possible, the recurrence of tragedies. For example, through the reform of regulatory frameworks for prevention, the funding of scientific research, investment in health facilities or other specific sectors, the construction of particular apparatuses for disaster management, and so on.

In short, in the contemporary age, marked by a general extension of state functions, state intervention in highly critical situations becomes essential. Still, its role should be it's equally decisive in absentia, when the public system fails to provide adequate responses and services, undermining the overcoming of the crisis.

If we refer to the Italian case, the earthquakes of 1976 in Friuli and 1980 in Irpinia provided two antithetical examples of excellent and lousy emergency management, although, paradoxically, the operational model that was initially put into practice was more or less the same. While in Friuli, the collaboration between the various institutional bodies and levels (central government, extraordinary commissioner, army, a regional body, local government, etc.) worked, allowing "not only to reduce the time of reconstruction but to relaunch the economy, strong from the renewed infrastructure built by the state," Irpinia became "the symbol of bad management of civil emergencies."

Already in the dramatic post-earthquake phase, there had been a severe delay in relief and aid; then, a perverse intertwining of politics, business, and the underworld developed in the subsequent period. The substantial resources invested in reviving the southern economy ended up in the hands of local syndicates, Camorra organizations, and unscrupulous entrepreneurs (including from the North).

On the other hand, as historian Piero Bevilacqua has observed, ever since the earthquakes of the early 20th century, public works and funding have become the instrument par excellence of extraordinary state intervention in Italy. Functioning as an "opportunity for redistribution of wealth from above," but to restore the pre-existing system of power and social order, rather than acting in depth to reshape class relations, reduce imbalances, and heal the economic and civil fabric.

The reaction to catastrophic events thus represents a kind of "litmus test" for assessing the mode and capacity of a state machine to function, but also for reflecting on the evolution of relations between political power and civil society.

Especially since, as various studies in social psychology explain, the attitude of communities affected by trauma changes over time. According to a centrifugal logic: while in the moment immediately following the explosion of the emergency, the tendency toward solidarity, cooperation, and collaboration with institutional actors prevails, bitterness, disillusionment, individualism, opportunism, resentment, and sometimes even anger emerge afterward, with an escalation that can result in violent social behavior.

It is easy then to witness the rapid resurfacing of divisions between political camps and within the social body, with a progressive polarization between private and public interests. In this way, the state to which hopes for an early recovery are initially entrusted can turn into a scapegoat.

The media system

The debate between public and private also exerts heavy pressure on the media system. First and foremost, the mass media as a whole offers a narrative of events that strongly influences the orientation of public opinion.

Depending on the degree of freedom of expression the political regime grants, this narrative may be, more or less, univocal or pluralistic. In republican Italy, although within a framework of general democracy, the reporting and interpretation of disasters have often been subordinated to political affiliation and carried out with instrumental intent.

An emblematic example was that of the Vajont in 1963, when almost all news outlets credited the official version, describing the disaster as a natural, imponderable and inescapable event caused solely by bad luck: a piece of mountain that landslides and falls into the reservoir of a dam and causes a flood on the valley below, overwhelming the inhabited centers. Only Tina Merlin, in the pages of the Communist Party's press organ "l'Unità," decided to fight to unveil the truth and denounce the responsibility of those who had wanted at all costs to carry out high-risk engineering work, ignoring opposing opinions. Then, but only thirty years later, it was a televised play that divulged to a broad audience the reality of a disaster that was anything but natural.

In more recent times, with the advent of the Internet and the transformations that the spread of the Net has imposed on the media information sector, disaster narratives have also undergone profound mutations, shattering into many communication streams. In Italy, as in the rest of the world, traditional media are sometimes forced into a subordinate role. Among other things, this has generated a problem of information hypertrophy that sometimes hinders the circulation of well-founded and reliable news.

In other words, it is increasingly within reach of many people to deepen their knowledge about emergency events occurring anywhere on the planet. It has become more challenging to navigate the chaos of online information and distinguish those seriously documented from its fakes.

That aspect has significant consequences on the formation of individuals' opinions, as well as on the behavior of citizens who experience crises.

The question of the responsibilities of media communication in the evolution of emergencies also emerged clearly in the course of the "health" catastrophe caused by the Covid-19 pandemic. Still, there has long been a heated debate about the role of the media and, in particular, the tendency for the spectacularization of disasters. In a famous essay published some 20 years ago, Susan Sontag questioned precisely this practice of staging the "pain of others" and the resulting emotional reactions of the public:

Witnessing calamities occurring in another country as a spectator is a characteristic and essential modern experience, the aggregate result of the opportunities that those highly specialized professional tourists known as journalists have been offering us for more than a century and a half. [...] "Blood on the front page" reads the tried-and-true guideline of tabloids and television news broadcasts that give flash information around the clock -- in the face of which we react with compassion, anger, curiosity, or approval as each misery is placed before our eyes.

Although Sontag was referring specifically to "the steady growth of information flows about the torments of war," her words nonetheless describe the media attitude toward "non-war" catastrophes. To quote the title of another seminal essay on the subject, "the spectacle of pain" attracts the public's attention and thus provides a prime resource for media communication.

However, precisely because the inexorable laws of spectacle prevail, media attention to disasters is limited in duration and fades as the intensity of the emergency phase wanes. Victims are slowly abandoned and forgotten, and what remains, if anything, is the reiteration of established stereotypes. Taking the example of the earthquakes in Friuli and Irpinia, one discerns in the prevailing media discourse the repetition of dichotomous representations that contrast the alleged northern efficiency with the cliché of the inert, idle, opportunistic, corrupt, and ignorant southerner.

According to a stereotypical interpretation that still finds circulation in media discourse, the failures of the reconstruction in Irpinia would, in short, be attributable mainly to the anthropology of the victims themselves, incapable of reacting and guilty of squandering public money. Proceedings of similar trivialization take place, among other things, on a global scale, even concerning the victims of disasters in poorer, "backward" countries. Those who are in a certain sense considered co-responsible for tragic events precisely because of their material and cultural living conditions, according to the idea that "by us," that is, in the Western world, "it could not have happened."

Memory

Another agent that plays an essential function in the history of emergencies is memory. "In some respects," Gabriella Gribaudi argues, "the memory of the disaster is similar to that of the victims of the air war" since everything is lost in an instant. Any traumatic experience of such intensity inevitably remains etched in the memories of those who lived through it. Private memories also represent the disaster as a point of rupture, a caesura in the linear unfolding of one's existence, operating a process of mythologizing the past whereby there was a before in which harmony prevailed and then chaos, despair, and mourning.

As in wars, moreover, alongside the individual memories of victims and witnesses, and then the composite and often divisive public memory, are layered the volatile memories of mere spectators who followed the events through the media. It is a variety of memories, often just as hypertrophic as media narratives, that hardly compose a discourse capable of uniquely permeating public opinion. But while "hot" post-conflict memories tend to keep the rate of internal conflict within communities high - generating that problem of "excess memory," about which so much has been argued -, memories of other catastrophes tend to "cool down," to remain alive and sensitive only to the victims.

Thus, a progressive and general oblivion is triggered - a problem of "short memory," concluded Salvatore Botta reconstructing the Italian case history - which also has repercussions on preventing new episodes. Thus, various studies on the anthropology of disasters have highlighted the irrational stubbornness of human communities not to leave dangerous places or to fail to take proper precautions, ignoring expert warnings and the memory of previous disasters. As Gianluca Ligi pointed out, "it is precisely these 'cultural' orientations, in the anthropological sense, that shape a community's social vulnerability to a certain type of extreme event." And it is when collective memory fades and loses its ability to preserve society from the emergency experiences it has already faced in the past, that the required contribution to reconstruction and historical knowledge becomes more pressing.

PART 2: WATER

Not much is more important than water or so easily forgotten. It is there at the turn of the tap. It is ready and usually reliable.

Drinking water generally does not give rise to much thought. It is the most straightforward substance on the planet. You would not stop to appreciate the safety of water or consider how you are promoting your well-being when you wake up thirsty and get out of bed for a quick drink. In essence, your body recognizes what doesn't always reach your intellect. Nothing is more imperative than water when it comes to maintaining your health.

Those unfamiliar with preparedness may never have thought that something of such slight complexity could require a reasonable degree of problem-solving. The more complicated nature of water becomes more apparent when one recognizes its role in survival and then understands how the family would cope if typical methods of ensuring safe supplies were exhausted. Time is always of the essence when the water is not there.

Accounting for drinking water is among the critical components of preparedness. It requires serious effort on the part of those planning for the consequences of a disaster. Safe water could become a matter of life and death for the unprepared. It is a basic necessity for living and, therefore, a top priority.

In addition to a lack of ability to maintain proper body temperature, a lack of fluids would lead more quickly to your death. The rule of three makes this clear. The rule offers only three days without water before a person succumbs.

Unfortunately, water is not a carefree contingency. It is heavy. It is cumbersome. If it is not purified in some way, the potential for contaminants will present a disease risk that would make life much more difficult. It is an area of preparation that presents some challenges. Filling a few giant jugs and moving on to the next planning area does not get the job done.

The lack of clean water and inability to purify would become a significant concern for those who fall into survival situations or are otherwise far from the safety and protection of established preparations at home. Physical difficulties would increase well in advance of three days if you could not find a safe source for drinking. Preppers planning their stay-at-home strategies would want to think about all the possibilities that could affect water availability and devise different solutions that could account for the family's needs.

Planning for water seems quite reasonable when broken down to the basics. A good plan would include:

- Storage.
- The ability to collect water.
- Methods to make potentially dangerous water safe to drink when needed.

Satisfying the water component of a sound preparedness plan requires a level of thinking that most fail to exercise.

A variety of disaster situations could hinder access to clean, potable water. Power outages could affect the ability of homes to draw from their wells. Extended and widespread outages could lead to significant problems for the unprepared. Store shelves would empty of bottled goods faster than you could imagine in such a circumstance.

Earthquakes could damage the municipal network. Water planning presents a wide variety of "what ifs?" to think about regardless of where you call home.

Floods are commonplace and most often contaminate drinking water sources of all-natural disasters. Floods also bring with them the real possibility of endangering public health. These are challenging situations for households, regardless of their size.

When flooding occurs, the encroaching waters carry bacteria, chemicals, sewage, oil, and other contaminants collected along the way in private wells and through public systems. Families cannot always count on a quick return to normalcy.

Those who draw from the wells should probably wait for some tests for contamination after the flood waters recede.

People lose fluids in a variety of ways, from sweating to breathing. Experts say that a typical person needs two to three liters of fluids daily to compensate for what the body loses as a matter of life. Those average requirements do not consider the water you would need to wash dishes or prepare meals if the typical supplies were not there. Those engaged in the hard work that characterizes survival or recovery situations would sweat much more than usual and, therefore, would need even greater fluid intake to maintain the proper balance.

It is interesting to think about how preppers would manage if their plans were limited to storage space only.

Thoughts might begin with assessing how much you could reasonably store for home recovery. The amounts needed for health and the space required to maintain it are not mentioned to overwhelm but simply to suggest that a good water plan is best achieved through various strategies. You might collect rainwater as a means of extending your contingencies. A prepper would then consider other options such as filtration and chemical disinfection methods that would allow you to make water safe when needed and wherever you are.

Ensuring safe and sufficient water requires a little knowledge and the right equipment. An alert prepper would always have some means to provide adequate and safe fluids in case you run out. Planning would extend beyond the house to the car. Having a well-constructed travel bag is wise, and water is an essential component. It would not necessarily take a disaster affecting thousands or millions of people to worry about where to get the next drink.

You could imagine any number of hypothetical situations that could put you at risk as far as water needs are concerned.

Thinking well about water and unveiling potential emergencies that would impact supplies is the first big step forward.

Our continuous need for fluids is what drives the problem. You could go several days without food if the situation called for it. It would be a very uncomfortable time, but your survival mindset would allow you to overcome the misery and make the other efforts necessary for your safety and well-being. The rule of three sets death at three weeks for those with nothing to eat.

No one can go without water, even for short stretches, without experiencing real health impacts. Loss of bodily fluids could quickly render you incapacitated and unable to move forward. Limiting a plan to a short-term supply is better than having no plan at all. Indeed, emergencies of three days or less are pretty every day and are more likely to impact families than a major disaster.

However, you should ask yourself how much you are willing to gamble with your family's safety. Your wellness clock starts ticking as soon as your water supply runs out. Someone working hard in hot conditions without access to fluids might begin to feel the first effects of dehydration in as little as an hour or two. There's a reason sporting events have all those Gatorade or Energade water bottles sitting courtside for athletes to draw from.

Three-day death is only part of the story when thinking about the urgency of water needs. The needs are immediate. The offered three-day rule suggests a little more leeway than you would have when dehydration problems set in. The rule glosses over the severe toll that lack of fluids has on the body all along the way.

Living is a relative term. Indeed, you may well be able to catch your breath while lying incoherent as the three-day mark without fluid intake approaches. Even after a day of no fluids, a person might struggle powerfully. Weakness and that general feeling of "sickness" could become a significant obstacle to safety in the early stages of dehydration. As the lack of fluids persists, you would move lower and lack the physical capacity to deal with all the other challenges that arise in a survival situation or following a disaster reasonably soon.

Maintaining good health requires paying more attention to what the body says rather than what the guidelines suggest.

You could have those three liters full and still encounter some dehydration problems. When working in disaster areas, it was typical to see charts reminding people to keep an eye on the color of their urine as a reliable guide to their hydration levels.

An adequately hydrated person has clear urine. More cloudy urine means you should drink more. The level of your water needs and the dangers presented by dehydration increase as the color becomes darker.

Right tools, the right know-how

Many people every year get sick from unintentional ingestion while swimming in public waters such as lakes, oceans, and sometimes even swimming pools.

The parasite Giardia lamblia is too common in natural waters, ponds, or even the clear trickling stream. It could become a problem in wells and municipal systems after the disaster. The parasite presents various issues, from stomach cramps and bloating to severe diarrhea. Cryptosporidium is another microorganism common to water and could cause diarrhea, stomach pain, nausea, and vomiting.

Those in survival mode would do well to stop and think about those illnesses if natural waters were to arouse temptations. Consuming contaminated water regardless of your extreme thirst could exacerbate your already high risks in a water emergency. Diarrhea and vomiting will significantly accelerate your body's dehydration. Dehydration occurs rapidly without the added boost of a parasitic disease.

The water component of the pack would include clean water to get through the day and ways to collect water and make it safe. Understanding the urgency of water, preppers would leave nothing to chance at home or elsewhere. Preppers away from home should have their bags handy and full of equipment to keep track of food, water, and shelter.

Those who collect from natural waters with the intent to purify should try to draw from running, rather than stagnant, sources if possible.

A pot and a heat source might be the easiest and most reliable way to ensure your water is safe to drink. Boiling would kill the various microorganisms that pose the most significant risks of waterborne diseases. Boiling the water for five minutes would generally eliminate the risks posed by bacteria and parasites. Those who live at higher altitudes would like to extend that time a bit. It is ready for consumption after it has cooled.

Some would argue that less than five minutes would make the water safe to drink. Some experts would say that one minute does a good job. The aftermath of a disaster or survival situation is not the right time to take unnecessary risks that could potentially make an already tricky situation disastrous. On the opposite end, you might remember that boiling for longer than necessary would only turn more of that water supply into escaping steam. Five minutes, it seems, provides a good compromise.

Some chemical means are available that increase your chances of safety when situations call for drinking from questionable sources. They are manufactured specifically for water purification and are generally available at sporting goods and camping stores. You might put away some iodine tablets in your travel bag or have a stash hidden in your car. It is a small, lightweight and inexpensive backup option, but it is also one that brings some cause for discomfort.

Iodine tablets effectively kill many dangerous bacteria, including E. coli. Iodine may still leave you at risk of cryptosporidium infection. It is not the most convenient or pleasant means of obtaining safe water. The method usually takes half an hour, and the iodine leaves a relatively strong taste.

Regular household bleach provides another way to disinfect. Like iodine pills, bleach does not provide a foolproof means of safety.

It improves your chances of avoiding disease. Chlorine bleach kills some but not all microorganisms that might present health risks.

The U.S. Environmental Protection Agency recommends boiling over bleach if it is an available option. If you rely on that method, you should mix well and let the water sit for half an hour before consumption. Those who rely on bleach put eight drops in 4 liters of water to disinfect it.

Cheap, ordinary bleach is best when it comes to water safety. Be careful to use regular, odorless bleach. It usually comes in at 5 to 5.25 percent chlorine concentration. As you can imagine, products with a safe color and pleasant smell are better suited for your laundry tasks than your drinking supplies.

The best tools for ensuring water safety require a small investment. Filter systems, whether for home or camping, would still do much to offer you peace of mind about the viability of your water plans. The best filters could turn the murkiest water into something clear, safe, and drinkable from a taste standpoint.

You would want to ensure that you are spending appropriately on high-quality products recognizing that it is a matter of family safety. You should read before you buy to ensure that the product you consider is reliable and capable of removing microorganisms and other contaminants. Many less expensive and readily available filtration units in most stores are designed to improve water taste rather than address contamination.

As for home systems, Berkey filters are highly valued by preppers and the survivor community. They have been shown to reduce contaminants to undetectable levels, whether viruses, bacteria, parasites, or harmful chemicals that could become a problem during a disaster. They are, however, expensive. Smaller models cost more than 200 dollars. Larger units would make much more sense if purchased with preparedness, mainly for a family of several people.

Those who prepare their travel bags should consider a hand-pump purification system. Pumps very reliably remove contamination from natural water sources. They produce clear, clean water that you could pump into a bucket or a camel backpack. The pumps cost between 100 and 300 dollars. This is money well spent for those who spend time outdoors and could prove invaluable should you end up in survival mode.

Many of the most popular filters designed for the home or travel bag have been known to do a truly outstanding job even with some pretty disgusting water. Still, it is in everyone's interest to use the cleanest water available.

At the very least, those who have resigned to using water laden with debris may want to run it through a gauze to remove the more significant bits of sediment. You might also want to run the water through semi-fold sand and gravel that would recreate soil filtration and accomplish the same. Filters get dirty faster without that little bit of care.

Those in water emergencies could use some of these methods to improve safety. Boiling, for example, would kill all those nasty bugs but would leave a difficult situation for the more taste-sensitive. Brown, foul-smelling water could be difficult for many people to digest. Boiling would offer some guarantees regarding pathogens. A filter would remove all other impurities, leaving the clear water that people are used to drinking. The same goes for removing the iodine and chlorine aromas left by tablets and bleach.

These solutions offer varying degrees of safety but also assume that safe water is readily available. Those who live in regions where water is not so abundant should have the necessary assets to create solar distillers stowed in their cars and travel bags. It does not take long and could become a lifesaver.

Solar stills are simple tools that rely on sunlight and condensation to draw clean, pure water from available soil or vegetation. Dry riverbeds offer ideal locations for installation as long as those in survival mode can find them. The first step, in that case, would require digging deep enough to find some moisture.

The still is a cup or some other form of the catch basin and a plastic sheet. You should put the cup in the hole and secure the plastic over the top with rocks or whatever is available to hold it.

From there, you would put a pebble in the plastic cup's center to create a conical shape. Sunlight does the rest of the work. Pure water evaporates from the sun's heat, leaving behind impurities. Those drops of pure, contaminant-free water stick to the plastic and drip into the cup. Some people run a straw under the plastic and into their catch basin so they can drink the water as it collects.

Those who cannot find dry river beds could fill the hole with as much vegetation as possible and similarly extract moisture from those plants.

Any moisture would be sufficient. You could urinate in the hole before you put the cup down and separate that little bit of water from the rest of its substance.

Time and quantity could present problems for those relying on solar distillers for collection.

Those who engage in preparedness would do well to keep some drinking water in their vehicles. It is critical to stay healthy if an accident, empty gas tank, or engine problems leave you in a place where you cannot expect immediate help. It is not unreasonable to think that you may find yourself out of reach of safety for several days. Without water, several days could also be an eternity.

You might consider your environment when extending plans and strategies to potential daily danger.

Those with a budget of $2,000 or more can turn to several online retailers specializing in survival and purchase full-year supplies of canned drinking water. The cans boast a 30-year shelf life. Like food, those packages represent only one person's needs. You certainly wouldn't need to spend that kind of money, particularly on a substance that regularly falls from the sky.

Store-bought containers, single-serve bottles, or jugs would offer the most convenient way to build your water supply.

They are safe, sealed, and ready for storage. Jugs are inexpensive, and you could build up your supply by putting a few more in your cart during your next weekly shopping trips.

Different experts have different opinions on shelf life. The U.S. Food and Drug Administration states that properly stored bottled water has an indefinite shelf life. The FDA notes that water may have an unpleasant odor or taste if it remains unopened too long.

There is a concern in some circles that chemicals from containers may begin to leach into the water over time and present some health problems. You can find "use by" dates on some bottled waters. Others suggest a shelf life of a year or two.

Those concerned about water quality and safety could rotate emergency supplies and use those bottles approaching "expiration" dates for daily consumption.

You could alleviate concerns by running water through a filter if you have not rotated and have an ample supply beyond expiration dates. Having several means to provide for safety takes away a lot of the stress that a water emergency must present.

Bottling from the tap is another option and even cheaper than that provided by the grocery store. You can use empty two-liter soda bottles or previously used water bottles. You could buy some 20-liter jugs that outgrow water coolers, whether or not there is a cooler to place them on.

You should thoroughly clean whatever container you choose with warm water and dish detergent. You could use a little bleach and water to sanitize. Adding a few drops of bleach to full containers would work well to prevent bacteria growth that would not be a problem with store-bought sealed products. Be sure to rinse well before using.

Preppers have many options when it comes to water. There is no perfect plan for everyone. However, water provides one of the most exciting portions of the project.

Nothing is more straightforward, but water's place in our lives is anything but. It makes up 71 percent of the earth's surface, although dying from lack of water is still a real threat.

The rule of three offers no leeway, so putting a solid plan in place is imperative. Having the methods to get safe water wherever you mean having the ability to avoid catastrophe. It is worth considering when filling the next glass.

Most of us think of "food and water" as unlimited resources. But if unprepared citizens were locked up in a shelter because of severe relapses, they would soon realize that they would have to prioritize adequate conserving water.

For the kidneys to effectively eliminate waste products, the average person needs to drink enough water to urinate at least half a liter a day.

When water is not limited, most people consume enough to urinate 1 liter. Additional water is lost in sweat, exhaled breath, and excreta). In cold conditions, a person could survive for weeks on 1.5 liters of water a day if they ate only a small amount of food and if that food was low in protein. However, cold conditions would be the exception in crowded underground shelters occupied for many days.

Under such circumstances, four or five liters of drinking water per day are essential when boiling, with no one allowed to wash. Fifty-five liters per person should be stored in or near a shelter for a two-week stay in a shelter. This amount would usually provide some remaining water after two weeks to prevent thirst should the dangers of relapse continue.

In a 1962 two-week Navy shelter occupancy test, 99 sailors consumed an average of 2.3 liters of water per day. The test was conducted in August near Washington, DC: the weather was unusually cool. The shelter was not air conditioned except during the last two days of the test.

When you sweat a lot and do not eat salty food, salt deficiency symptoms, particularly cramps, are likely to develop within a few days. To avoid this, you should consume foods and drinks 6 to 8 grams of salt daily.

If little or no food is eaten, this small daily ration of salt should be added to the drinking water. In hot conditions, a little salt improves the taste of water.

Water sources

Given the incredible number of rivers, streams, and lakes, you would think that finding water would not be a problem.

Unfortunately, pollution and elemental contamination have rendered many of these sources useless. Although they can be used after purification, you may often need a more ready source.

The best source of pure water is rain.

Prepare a cistern or jar during rain and collect as much as possible. Rainwater is generally free of contamination and will quench your thirst.

If that fails, try ice: once it has melted, it is always safer to drink than anything from a river.

Please, stay in alert: in the event of a nuclear disaster, these water sources will be radioactive, and filtering or purifying them will be almost impossible.

In this extreme case, dig for water in muddy areas. You will have to filter it through a cloth, but this water table is generally safe.

Finally, you will probably have to take a supply of ready-to-drink water in sachets or bottles. However, remember that this source is limited, and you must consider a long-term solution such as purification.

Water purification

Purification can quickly turn river or lake water into something useful.

You have only one purification choice when it comes to a prepper's bag: purification tablets.

These tablets are generally iodine-based, easy to use, and can purify about one liter of water per tablet.

In addition, you can also boil water, although it is time-consuming and requires a great deal of energy, not to mention that you will not purify radioactive water by boiling it. Tablets are much better.

Water filtration

The filtration process is another option. These mechanical options can give you safe drinking water, though usually at the expense of your energy.

A hand-pumped filter will allow you to filter enough water to last for weeks, while a simple survival straw will keep you going almost as long.

Become familiar with how both work and store the filter in your bag if you have room. Otherwise, it becomes an essential part of your car kit while the straw will go in your vehicle's bag.

Avoid commercial products such as filtered water bottles. They are designed to work with tap water, not water from puddles, rivers, streams, or lakes.

PART 3: FOOD AND HOW TO STORE IT

Food planning and storage, when considered from the place of preparation, provides another interesting example of how much society has changed in the last half-century. It is a topic that those who are new to preparation might find a significant departure from their daily lifestyle. In reality, however, the idea of having a good amount of food on hand to ensure that the family can meet its long-term needs is not new.

Many of the efforts undertaken by preppers today to ensure that the family had enough to eat after the disaster were daily chores only a few generations ago. Until recently, food required much more thought and effort, even in the short term. It was not that far back when having only a week's worth of food on hand could have caused families some deep concerns.

Today, a week's worth of groceries is the norm. There are more options now than there were then. We have things more accessible, although it is wise to think of the future today as it has always been. If disaster strikes, the prepared family with a good supply of food at home will be much more comfortable than the family that hopes and waits for help without good guarantees.

Believe it or not, many people still live with a long-term sensitivity regarding food. Preppers, among many others, will plant extensive gardens and do some canning at harvest time just as their ancestors did.

If they are lucky in the field, hunters always have a good supply of game in the freezer. It provides meals throughout the year and until the next season arrives. It is the way people have always lived.

Modern technology has made long-term preparation much easier than it was for our grandparents. Some preppers will rely heavily, sometimes exclusively, on shelf-stable products that are commercially available, either because of lack of space in the house, ability, or interest in using older methods of food storage. Canned foods, freeze-dried foods, dry cereals, and other products remain viable for years and often decades. They allow the family to eat well and without worry; if a disaster should panic, the community as grocery stores begin to empty.

Planning at those levels might seem strange to those who have never known anything other than fulfilling their weekly shopping lists. It is more a function of our society's short memory. Long-term food storage dates back to the earliest history of human civilization. Technology has simplified everyday life, but it has come at the expense of readiness for the unpredictable.

Food, for many in the modern era, has become an afterthought. It is a grab-and-go society. You eat when you're hungry and don't have to make much effort to get a meal. The drive-in along the road is often seen as cheap and reliable when time is short or food is scarce. In urban and suburban settings, fast food restaurants are rarely more than a few minutes from home.

That all too familiar relationship with food would open the door to some severe problems in the event of a disaster. Those whose meal plans and habits do not go beyond trips to restaurants and keep some essential foods in their kitchens are setting themselves up for starvation in an emergency.

Our grocery stores, ironically, like most of the people they serve, do not stock up on long-term supplies. Store shelves can become bare fairly quickly when disasters or even panic caused by short-term emergencies impact a community (think sunflower seed oil).

History has shown that preppers do not deal with the undocumented and the hypothetical when it comes to long-term food planning, even in our modern era. Those unfamiliar with preparation may think about spending even a few uncomfortable days without a decent meal. The stores are empty.

Accounting for food needs in the wake of the disaster requires a shift from the modern, commonsense approach to eating. Many people take food for granted, and it is not so difficult to understand why during a typical day. You can and should enjoy the wonders of modern convenience. The dangers begin to settle when people rely too much on all the ease it offers.

The rule of three

Although potential emergencies vary from place to place, those facing preparedness have a fundamental tool to work with that allows anyone to consider and construct appropriate survival plans, regardless of circumstances.

Well-designed plans provide comfort during emergencies, but surviving is the primary goal. It does not require a degree in biology to recognize that the human body will not last too long without food or water.

This is where the rule of three comes in. The rule-a list of the fundamental factors that affect your ability to survive establishes the top priorities and serves as the very foundation of any reasonable planning effort. As grim as it may sound, it is a list that quickly lays out the basics of being prepared.

<u>According to the rule, you can live:</u>

Three minutes without air

Three hours without shelter

Three days without water

Three weeks without food

Three months without hope

These are the three central components of the 5 rules that should attract the most attention when you start assembling your preparations. I hope someone is not underwater and struggling to find the surface for three minutes. In that situation, preparation efforts would not be applicable. Also, no tool or strategy would help if you were hopeless for a long time.

When considered in terms of the rule, "shelter" does not necessarily refer to a structure or a roof over our heads. It refers to any means to keep ourselves clean and maintain a healthy body temperature. For example, the possibility of starting a fire would fall under the shelter category.

Regarding water, let's start with a fundamental thought: where would the many unprepared among us go to get our daily necessities without all those taps that make life so easy? Often, emergencies interrupt people's ability to draw from their wells or disrupt their connections to municipal systems in our urban areas. Water problems could become a real emergency. Situations could arise where contaminated water flows through pipes and could cause disease if consumed. Water storage and the ability to collect safe water are among the top priorities of a good preparedness plan.

The rule of three requires thinking about how and what you would eat if a disaster left nearby grocery stores closed. The law prioritizes food, but remember that it only talks about how long you could live without it. Keeping a pulse and maintaining health and well-being are two very different things. Those preparing should consider their own dietary needs while also considering how many others would need to be feed.

Because it talks about basic survival needs, the rule of three provides only one-half of the integral equation. The other side lies in applying your ability to walk that basic survival map for various periods if any emergency calls for it. The rule keeps moving forward.

Suppose a disaster situation is short-term, spanning three days or less. Those with minimal preparedness could find themselves in difficult, stressful, though manageable, situations. It could be that a severe storm knocked down trees and power lines, leaving a mess in the yard and a widespread series of problems for the power company to manage. In that case, the preparedness series is not as critical to staying alive but could do much to provide relief until normalcy returns.

Short-term outages that get in the way of everyday life would still require common sense and thought. Those who make it through that three-day power outage, for example, would do well to eat things out of the refrigerator and freezer first to make sure their food supplies don't go wrong. The typical unprepared family would encounter natural stress but would make it through.

The family would probably be fine with food if a short-term emergency fell before a typical shopping day. A house with any degree of insulation would allow a family to meet shelter needs, even if not in capacities beyond blankets and sweatshirts. Those who do not keep additional water for emergencies might have more difficult times, but in the short term, they would still have enough liquid on hand.

As emergencies linger, it becomes more critical for people to have solid contingencies. The level of preparedness amid emergencies becomes more urgent every day. Every day a disaster hinders a usual way of life, and more people have to rely on themselves and their environment just as people did in earlier eras.

Three days provides the magic number to consider when assembling preparations. It is a psychological benchmark. At that point, thoughts shift from the confidence that a situation will end fairly quickly to the brutal realization that life may be challenging for a while. These worries diminish in equal proportion to your planning. At that point, however, the rule of three also begins to play at a much more significant level.

Three days is a fairly reliable indicator of when a situation goes from merely uncomfortable to presenting real difficulties for those without adequate preparations. Many would begin to have a wrong time at that point.

Sanitation, for example, could become a critical issue for many unprepared families if recovery from the crisis lasted from three days to a few weeks. Morale and self-confidence could decline for some if the house leaks water and the family cannot flush by normal means. It is one of the many areas of our daily lives that is not given much thought. People understand its importance better when that luxury is not there.

The critical issue, however, is the same for all: those unable to secure potable water are at serious risk.

To survive, an average person must consume about 2 liters of fluids daily. Most short-term plans would not be sufficient because the days keep passing. Those with only a few jugs of drinking water stashed away for emergency use would run out of supplies quickly.

Concerns diminish as the plans get deeper. Thinking step by step about water challenges would open up other options besides having a few 4-liter jugs tucked away. "I have a tub from which I could draw water to flush or wash dishes," she says. "I could run that water through a filter to allow for drinking if needed."

Some would have settled for other contingencies. Many do not have large tubs or pools.

Going through that thought process shows that no matter where you live, you can find ways to put your family in a better position to handle a potential disaster. It is simply a matter of untangling how a disaster would hinder the way we as people usually live and finding ways to explain them. Water is just one piece of the puzzle.

Many preppers out there have food supplies packed that could feed a family for several months. Transitioning from a few weeks of struggle to a matter of months would require much effort from even the most prepared person. After so long, you would have to take on a completely different mindset and focus on sustainable living.

That is not unreasonable.

A plan that goes beyond the period of several months to a year or more is no longer about preparedness. If you were to rely on your assets and equipment for more than a year, the idea of preparedness should give way to a recognition that the community needs to work together for the greater good. At that point, you should step back in time and recognize the family's need to hunt, grow food, gather water, and find shelter as people did 150 years ago.

It is frightening to think about that level of disaster, particularly when compared with the recovery periods after even the most devastating events that have recently happened.

A period of up to a few months is a good sign to keep in mind when developing preparations. Disaster inflicts more damage on some than others, but in a community sense, most events involve only interruptions that could affect survival for up to a few weeks. Many preppers wisely assemble the necessary equipment and supplies to handle more prolonged periods. As is often said, prevention is better than cure.

Building a solid plan takes time and work. It will also cost some money. Anyone who has to stick to a family budget can still carry out the preparation.

When applying risks and worst-case scenarios to the rule of three, preppers will inevitably come across several ideas that make a lot of sense for their families. A prepper, for example, would probably want a large, durable tent in case the worst-case event compromises the home or forces a quick evacuation. Even in minor scenarios, those aiming for comfort might want camping lanterns or oil lamps to provide easy and reliable light sources.

Crank radios have become famous for obtaining vital information on hazards, damage, and recovery efforts. Radios could also provide some entertainment when the power goes out. You should not neglect to own a few things on hand that can provide some entertainment and reduce stress.

In many ways, solid plans come together through a series of lower costs. Assembling an excellent first aid kit makes sense and will not ruin the bank account. Those concerned about spending should take the time to honestly assess needs against the rule of three and then prioritize.

Some instruments would require a fairly substantial investment. A 5,000-watt generator starts at about 500 dollars. It would allow the family to keep the freezer running, use the water filtration pump, and run a heater. After a good and honest evaluation, attention to cost might determine that a few car batteries and a small inverter would be sufficient to meet emergency power needs.

Many preppers address at least part of their food contingencies by purchasing military ready-to-eat meals. They are an easy and reliable option since they provide substantial calories and generally have five years or more shelf life. It is not—however, a cheap option to take.

A 12-pack meal costs about 65 dollars. Some may look for other less expensive and shelf-stable options.

Preparation is a process that can certainly be as expensive as you want to make it. The costs increase with the time you spend trying to provide for self-sufficiency. If you have a goal of going from zero to fully stocked and able to meet three months of needs, you're going to have to spend money.

You should not feel the need to do this. It might be a matter of getting the best value for money by satisfying a series of smaller but essential purchases before tackling the more expensive items. As you make the smaller purchases, you might set aside a few dollars and slowly accumulate them toward the price of a generator, a water filtration unit, or the cost of having a wood stove installed in your home.

The critical point is that everyone can prepare. It is important to remember that the first and most crucial component of any solid preparation plan does not cost a dime. It is learning, thinking, and having the ability to break down potential problems.

Step one: a survival mindset

The essential tool available during the preparation process and after a disaster is not available for purchase at the local hardware store. Each of us received one for free. It is the brain. The first goal is to use that extraordinary tool to its total capacity. It starts with recognizing that nothing can be taken for granted. You should realize how quickly you can run into some severe problems.

Many people have dramatic ideas about what it would take to put someone in a position to fight for survival. In reality, it doesn't take much. It could be as simple as running out of gas during the winter while driving on a country road. That driver could go into survival mode if the heater didn't work, and there was a severe possibility that another car wouldn't pass for a while.

Preparation is a matter of recognizing your possible problems and limitations. It is a matter of finding the correct answers and the right attitude. Preparation will make life easier after a disaster, but it will not make life easy. The best equipment in the world could not make a difference to the person who does not have the will or drive to face the worst that nature or manufactured disasters could bring.

Those who are unable to secure potable water are at serious risk. Rain barrels are easy to collect and store water to meet that need.

The main point is that the equipment alone does not leave you prepared. Planning requires strategy. It starts and ends with the all-important tool between our ears.

You should recognize that the best supplies are meaningless if their goods are not accessible. Someone stuck in the woods could not rely on their three-day survival kit if they left it in the closet at home.

Preppers have to think about every little problem in a disaster. You could pull out your equipment and set up camp if the worst happened.

It is easy to fall short in planning by failing to think through a problem to its conclusion.

A small survival kit in the glove compartment of your vehicle may be a burden until you need it. Plan ahead.

As plans develop, confidence will also grow.

Principles of preparedness would serve a family well as a community struggles against any wake of calamity. It does not mean that your thoughts and efforts should be hidden and left to the time of need. An attitude of self-reliance has its place in everyday life as well.

Self-sufficiency in food means having a livelihood on hand that goes beyond what was bagged at the supermarket over the weekend. The food component of a good preparedness plan could make good economic sense for a family even in typical daily life. You could use space and half an hour a day to take care of a good-sized garden.

Growing food is inexpensive and lends itself to a healthy lifestyle. You might not grow vegetables for a whole year, but even a few months of food is worth it. Gardening requires some space, but many could accomplish it even with smaller properties.

Some of those who live in the city may determine that the well-maintained garden offers nothing more than a weekly mowing job. That space could be better used as a garden. Those who live in rural areas would find that it is essential to raise chickens. They provide perfect protein in the form of eggs every week.

Self-sufficiency goes beyond food. It comes down to the little things. Those who engage in preparation often find that it is not something separate from the rest of their lives. It simply becomes part of their way of life.

Lamps are great tools from a preparer's point of view because they provide light and don't create warmth.

There are many opportunities to take what you are already doing and make it part of your preparation. Those who barbecue as a hobby could read and experiment and quickly learn how to smoke fish. It would open up a great source of stored protein if a disaster impacted the food supply.

Hunters are not heading into the field hoping to add their skills to long-term plans, but they are doing just that. Those who enjoy gardening practice self-sufficiency but may not see it that way. It's just part of their lifestyle. The hobbyist with basic car repair skills has a solid self-sufficiency skill that could come in handy quickly during an emergency.

Preparation at first requires thought and effort that many have not considered before. It will become more natural. As the process progresses, preppers will find that it has just become part of who they are. Preppers become more self-sufficient as the preparations unfold, manifesting in their daily lives.

Living in preparedness offers peace of mind when we understand the risks around us. Extending your self-sufficient attitude beyond worries about what might happen makes much sense. Those who live with their preparations may be less stressed when problems hit. They are already able to handle them in a calm and well-considered way.

Preparedness requires equipment and supplies, but it is much more practice in mindset. As you develop a self-sufficient attitude, the ideas of "survival" and "preparedness" become more negligible. The understanding of preparedness as "just our way of life" grows in equal measure.

Begin food planning

To get food planning off to a good start, it is necessary to consider how long the family intends to be self-sufficient. Some are comfortable with an emergency food supply that would feed the family for a month. Others will assemble and store a food cupboard that represents three months of meals.

There is no right or wrong answer overall. The risks vary from country to country. Even people living in the same region would have different degrees of comfort. You might have less confidence than another in the ability of society at large to restore food supplies in a hurry. Some people out there want to be ready for doomsday. Everyone is different.

The frequency of short- and medium-term emergencies suggests the real risk of having less than several weeks' worth of food ready for use at any given time. After reaching that minimum, you should build your storage cabinet according to your concerns. That is a process that should be undertaken for some reason. You should not overburden your family finances to reach the desired threshold.

Many preppers suggest that having a food cupboard covering a few months is quite reasonable. Major disasters have certainly impacted community food supplies for long periods. The family with the food cupboard built for a month or less could run out of stores too quickly after highly destructive events.

On the other hand, some would argue that food plans that extend beyond a year only serve to delay the inevitable should something happen, that would require using that entire supply. If the stores are down for that long, you might assume they won't return. At that point and earlier, you would want to try to plant and hunt or potentially raise animals for subsistence, just as people did in the old days.

The next big question is how much food you would need for the family. Preparing should consider what the family eats daily when planning supplies to meet the chosen times. Pay attention to typical consumption and buy enough to allow family members to increase caloric intake as needed during recovery. Your regular diet may not be sufficient based on a disaster's aftermath's stress and physical requirements.

For example, an average 40-year-old sedentary man would need 2,400 calories to balance his intake with the energy his body would burn to live. The same man, if active, would need 2,800 calories to meet the needs of bodily function and that added exertion.

Women generally require less food than men. The average, sedentary 40-year-old woman would need 1,800 calories. Her active counterpart would require 2,200 to maintain a healthy balance. Caloric needs tend to peak for men and women in their late teens and early 20s. Active men in their 20s and 30s typically require 3,000 calories daily, while their female counterparts would need about 2,400.

For several reasons, those planning food storage to account for disaster should aim for the higher end of the calorie charts. It will take more than light meals (salads would not be enough) to adequately fuel the body when doing heavy work that is not part of the routine.

After a disaster, you would have to deal with exertion and the body working in ways it is not used to. You might stress muscles that don't work much on an average day. There may be trees to cut and wood to carry. You may have to tackle some of your roofing work or repair other damage left to the family home.

Your energy production could extend beyond muscle considerations, depending on the circumstances. Winter emergencies could put families in limited heat situations.

MREs, a standard package for preppers, suggest that caloric intake for the typical day and the average man or woman would not be sufficient for the highly active. The meals are designed for and used by soldiers but are readily available to the civilian community. Each one comes in at more than 1,200 calories. The sedentary man or woman should not take three a day for any time if he or she is trying to maintain a slim life.

Those who plan their food supplies should equally rely on logic and common sense in planning quantities beyond the usual. The real point of conservation is to overcome any period that would present an inability to restock the shelves. It is a much better position to recognize that you may be over-prepared than to watch food supplies dwindle when the community has not yet recovered.

Good plans will include fruits, vegetables, grains, and protein sources.

There is a fundamental difference when buying long-term. Your potential food selections become much narrower. The store's deli, baked goods, and bakery sections will not do much for the long-term shopper. You have to pay attention to how long those foods will survive on the shelf. Expiration dates take on a much greater level of importance. It requires a good strategy.

It is critical to have enough food. It is equally crucial to have the right food.

Many people have chest freezers in the basement. They are good appliances from the standpoint of extending the family's food supply. However, you should not consider those frozen foods as part of your long-term emergency provisions.

The freezer in the basement would surely be able to meet the family's needs quite well in the shortest possible time. In case of loss of electricity, the freezer would become the immediate priority of meal planning.

Preppers who buy long-term must think differently, but many options are still available to allow a person to eat well enough. You should not have to survive on rice and water alone. The number of foods that will hold up over the long term is becoming more abundant.

There are many different ways to approach a proper food plan. Those seeking the ultimate convenience could get everything they need to feed their family for an entire year without leaving their properties.

Several companies offer annual packages of freeze-dried and canned foods with a shelf life of 25 years or more. They are specially assembled to provide some variety and take the guesswork out of building a preparation plan. It is a viable option for some people, although it is not hard to imagine that the price factor would push many toward other possibilities.

Many of the boxes on the market are not unreasonable in terms of cost when broken down by meal. Packages start at about $1,000 and can go up to $3,000. Packages, meanwhile, are usually put together per person. Some are comparable to what people would spend weekly on food for the family.

What becomes unreasonable for many people is the idea of building a whole year's worth of other food that will be hidden, lurking, and paid for in a significant, solitary transaction. That would not work for many people's budgets.

Many foods a family typically buys for everyday life would hold up perfectly for several years. Canned products are a good example. The canning process involves using high heat to kill bacteria in the food and creating a vacuum seal to prevent new bacteria from entering. Bacteria are what cause food spoilage.

Many commercially canned products remain viable for long periods. A preparer might take note of "use by" dates and keep an eye out for dates that extend over long periods.

Dry and freeze-dried foods offer years and sometimes decades of shelf life. Powdered milk and eggs would provide a long shelf life and the nutrition and comfort of having those staple foods on hand regardless of whether they are available in fresh form. Dried beans would last forever as long as they are stored properly. They would provide families with another source of protein to draw from.

Pressure canning

Many people carry out the so-called home sterilization of jars that will later hold tomatoes, cucumbers, pickles, fruit sauces, jellies, etc.

It was Louis Pasteur who, shortly after the mid-1800s, could examine how by subjecting wine to a temperature of 6°F for a certain amount of time, it could be preserved for a more extended period.

It is essential to remind the origin of this crucial sanitization technique, which is still applied on various food matrices, allowing the killing of both pathogenic and non-pathogenic microorganisms (i.e., all microbial forms, including spores).

Let's start with this: dry heat is less effective than moist heat. Steam is considered an effective disinfectant because any resistance outer the protective layer of microorganisms can be "softened," allowing them to die. For example, for Clostridium botulinum, an extremely dangerous pathogen in canned food, the spores of this bacterium are broken down in about five minutes at 250°F by using saturated steam. On the contrary, achieving a similar effect with forced ventilation (dry air) oven would require raising the temperature to about 60°F.

It should be remembered that the classical sterilization system is based on the principle used by homemakers for jams and preserves. The main difference between the industrial method is the higher temperature achieved thanks to the autoclave, which, by allowing the working pressure to be increased, allows the boiling temperature of water to be raised above 200°F, bringing it above 250°F for 30 minutes.

A pressure stove, used at home for cooking, can be seen as a small autoclave, similarly operating with pressurized steam at a given temperature can sterilize jars that will later hold jams, vegetables, and so on.

I won't hide from you that in writing this book, I thought back to the actions my grandmother used to perform when in the summer, she would carefully prepare and sterilize on the stove in a pot the jars that would later store fruits and vegetables from the garden throughout the winter.

The pressure cooker or the microwave oven can be used for home sterilization. The former allows you to reach about 250°F and requires approximately 30 minutes for the process to be effective.

Before proceeding, we need to take a step back and understand the latter and its principle of operation.

In a regular pot, water boils around 212°F; the water vapor that is formed evaporates by diffusing into the air. Based on chemistry and physics, we know that high pressures increase the boiling point of water. Suppose we could make the air above our pot be at a much higher pressure than usual, allowing the water to boil at a considerably hotter temperature and thus cook our food faster.

This is the principle behind the pressure cooker, invented by Frenchman Denis Papin and perfected over the years. It is a large pot constructed of steel and fitted with a tight-fitting lid. The cover contains a thick rubber gasket that seals between the bottom of the lid and the top edge of the pot to achieve a "tight seal."

With a traditional pot, once 200°F is reached, the water evaporates; with a pressure cooker, the seal and lid hold the steam. Finding no way to vent the pressure inside the pot increases rapidly.

Although visually, the water inside the pot boils, given the increased pressure, the boiling temperature is higher, and the direct consequence is that the food cooks faster.

A unique safety valve on the top of the lid allows a small amount of steam to escape, preventing the pressure from reaching extreme values that would cause the pot to explode. If the pressure inside the pot reaches a critical level, the valve quickly opens, lowering the pressure back to a safe level.

It should be remembered that cooking in a pressure cooker improves the food's nutritional characteristics, positively impacting heat-sensitive water-soluble vitamins, B-group vitamins, and vitamin C (ascorbic acid). This method also prevents the formation of harmful volatile compounds during product processing.

The absence of air (thus oxygen) and light decrease the oxidation of vitamins and their precursors (beta-carotene) and fatty acids, the availability of which under normal conditions would be reduced or otherwise altered.

But back to our sterilization of the empty jars that will later go on to hold jams, sauces, etc., it will be necessary to:

Wash the glass jars and lids thoroughly with hot water and soap (liquid dish soap is perfect), remembering to rinse with hot water to remove any soap residue. Alternatively, you can wash the containers directly in the dishwasher.

Pay attention to jars with cracks (possibly with your hand, check that the rim of the jar is smooth and not chipped). In case of damaged jars, provide for their replacement.

The sterilization operation will be necessary even if the jars are new to remove any dust and contaminants accumulated during storage.

Loosen the ring at the top of each jar and leave them that way, as if pressure builds up inside the jar, it could cause it to explode.

Place the empty jars inside the pressure cooker, arranging them on the bottom but be careful to leave enough space between each jar so that there is no contact between them.

Fill the pot with water, exceeding the top edge of the jars by at least an inch. Deposit the pressure cooker lid and secure it.

Leave the closed pot containing the jars on the stove for 30 minutes. The drain valve must remain open long enough to allow the air contained in the pot to evaporate; when pure steam begins to form, it will be possible to close the drain valve.

This measure is intended to ensure proper pot use; if air remained inside, adequate sterilization temperatures could not be achieved.

A further reminder of this theory: the boiling point of water depends on pressure; the higher the pressure, the higher the boiling temperature. Therefore, the steam developed will be hotter, and the more effective the decrease will be.

When we hear the whistle due to the escape of excess steam from the valve, it will mean that the desired maximum pressure during our home sterilization process will have been achieved. Since boiling has begun, minimizing the flame will be possible.

At this point, it will be necessary to lower the pressure with the release valve by raising a lever or loosening a cap (depending on the model) and opening all the air and steam exhaust taps. In this way, the steam will escape, and the pressure will be lowered until it equals atmospheric pressure (it is obvious that the inside of the pressure cooker remains sterile until this is opened).

Let the jars cool for a few minutes and carefully remove them (be careful, do not speed up the cooling by, for example, putting the pot under cold tap water, mind you!) using special rubber-coated tongs and place them on a cloth to dry. After which all we have to do is fill the jars with food, replace the lids and screw on the new one.

If the jars are not filled right away, it will be wise to leave them in hot water until you are ready to serve them so that they remain sterile until the food is added.

Water Bath Canning

Preserves, whether fruit or vegetable, meat or fish, are food preparations made in airtight containers (screw cap or "hinged" closure) and subjected to heat treatments such as pasteurization and sterilization. Once ready, these preserves will keep for 1-5 years at room temperature in dark, dry, and well-ventilated places. The best container at home is the glass jar, preferably a half-liter jar, to facilitate pasteurization operations: it does not absorb odors, can be used several times, and is easily washed.

Before preparing the preserves, the chosen jars and their caps must be washed thoroughly and sanitized by boiling them in a water bath (the water must be at least 2 inches above the cap). Metal caps and lids with deformations, dents, and signs of rust or corrosion should be replaced to ensure the closure is airtight. It should be remembered that boiling may not be sufficient to destroy the spores of some bacteria, such as those of Clostridium botulinum, which should not germinate (for example, by increasing the acidity of the preserve): this is why it is referred to as sanitization and not sterilization. If the jars are hot-filled, they can be soaked in water at a temperature close to that of preparation. Otherwise, they should be dried thoroughly before filling.

Once the jars have been prepared, it is time to take care of the foods to be stored. Fruits and vegetables should be adequately ripened and similar in size, removing bruised or rotten parts, cores, stones, and peel when needed. The raw materials should be washed under running water and left in water and baking soda for a few minutes. If fruits from the home garden are used, it is advisable to prepare preserves within 6 to 12 hours of harvest or keep the product refrigerated.

When preparing jams, it is best to follow recipes that call for equal amounts of sugar to the fruit.

At this point, the steps to be performed vary depending on the type of preparation. To make jams, after cutting the fruit into small pieces, you need to add sugar, preferably white or caster cane sugar, because it does not alter the flavor and aroma of the fruit or jam sugar that contains pectin. The fruit and sugar mixture is brought to a boil, stirring and removing any foam, taking care not to let the sugar caramelize. In jams, the fruit thickens due to the pectin content a natural substance found in fruit which turns into gelatin during cooking. Pectin extracted from the fruit can be used for preparation.

When the cooking is finished, the containers should be hot-filled to 1-2 centimeters from the rim, after which they are turned upside down and allowed to cool. After 12 to 24 hours, the closure's airtightness and the vacuum attainment must be evaluated. Metal caps should appear slightly curved inward, and no "click clack" should be heard. For containers equipped with hinged caps and rubber gasket, the check is done by removing the safety catch and opening the lid by applying light pressure: if the lid does not resist, it means that the preserve is not vacuum-sealed.

The preservation of jams is influenced mainly by acidity and sugar content. As for acidity, it is advisable to add lemon juice if low-acid fruits are used. On the other hand, as for sugar, recipes in which it is used in quantities equal to those of the fruit are preferred, but in any case, it is best not to go below 700 g per kilogram of fruit. If overcooking causes sugar crystallization, which can be hindered by increasing acidity, undercooking makes the product too liquid and easily attacked by molds and microorganisms. There are two tests to determine if the jam is ready: by pouring a drop onto a plate (this should slide slowly, adhering to the surface), or by dipping and lifting a spoon into the mixture, the jam should have a sticky, stringy consistency.

If vegetable preserves are to be made, a distinction must be made between pickles. Before making a jar of pickled vegetables, chopped vegetables should be soaked and then cooked in a solution of water and vinegar in equal parts to acidify the product (spices and herbs should also undergo the same treatment). The vegetables should be left "al dente," drained, cooled, and dried, then placed in the container filling all available space but without crushing them too much. At this point, it is time to cover them entirely with oil, preferably an extra virgin, taking care not to leave air bubbles.

Once the jars are filled, it is necessary to proceed with the pasteurization of the preserves. The treatment must be carried out by completely submerging the jars in pots filled with water and at least 10 cm taller than the containers. The preserves should be boiled continuously, evenly, vigorously, and without interruption in the pot closed with the lid. If the water level drops, boiling water must be added, taking care not to pour it directly onto the jars. The time required for proper pasteurization (measured from the beginning of boiling) depends on the type of preserve, the type of container, and its size. Five to 10 minutes after the completion of pasteurization, the jars should be allowed to cool either wrapped in a wool blanket or directly in water. The next day, it will be necessary to check the tightness of the caps, as with jams. Jars in which a vacuum has not been created can be pasteurized again by changing the cap.

Pickles and pickled vegetables must undergo pasteurization once the jar is filled.

Vegetables preserved in this way may absorb some of the oil and therefore need to be topped up; however, the pasteurization step must be repeated. Over the next 10 to 15 days, the jar should show no signs of alteration, such as air bubbles or opalescence of the oil. Preserves must be consumed at least 2-3 months after preparation to appreciate the taste better. If the preparation methods have been carried out correctly, the storage time can be very long, even a year and a half.

As for pickles, vegetables can be either blanched in water, leaving them "al dente," or stored raw. It is preferable to use a 50-50 mixture of white wine vinegar (with an acidity level of 6 percent or more) and water or wine. Apple cider vinegar should not be diluted with water because it has a lower acidity level. Once the jar is filled, vinegar is added and pasteurized, as with pickled vegetables.

Jams and pickles are just a few of the many preserves that can be made at home covered by the ISS Guidelines. They also mention, for example, fish preparations, which are widespread, especially in some Italian regions. Great care must be taken when preparing salted fish: anaerobic conditions (absence of oxygen) can form in the lower layers of the preserve, which favor the development of botulinum, especially if the salt has not penetrated deeply into the fillets. To ward off bacterial growth, you must keep low temperatures during the early stages of preparation.

Precautions should also be taken in the preparation of canned marinated fish: in this case, bacterial growth is prevented by acidifying the product (raw or cooked), which is first immersed in brine with water and wine vinegar (or lemon) in the refrigerator, and then stored in oil. To block Clostridium botulinum's proliferation, you must achieve a pH of 4.5 or lower in the canned food.

It should be remembered that it is highly inadvisable to make natural preserves of vegetables, meat, and fish at home, which require an industrial sterilization process.

Just as it is hazardous to prepare pesto in oil at home, it is best frozen in convenient portions.

Water Bath canning explained step by step.

Below I will guide you through the whole process, step by step. But first, you should gather your supplies. Here is what you will need.

Supplies needed to sterilize canning jars:

Canning jars

Hot water

Water bath canner or other large pot

Soapy water

Dish brush or clean dish cloth

Canning jar lifter or regular kitchen tongs

White vinegar (optional)

Steps for preparing and sterilizing canning jars:

I will first provide a quick overview of the steps for your reference, then go into detail for each one below. Here are the steps for sterilizing canning jars.

Fill the water bath tray

Inspect the jars for any defects

Wash the jars in soapy water

Rinse clean jars with hot water

Place hot jars in the boiling water canner

Cover the jars with water

Boil them for 10 minutes to sterilize them

Step 1: Fill the pot with water: It takes a while before a large pot of water boils, so plan.

The first thing I do is fill the water bath pan with hot water and turn it on high, so it can start boiling while I work to clean the jars.

Step 2: Add vinegar to the water (optional): After using the jars a few times, you may notice a white film collecting on them. This is entirely normal and nothing to worry about.

To remove it, I add about 1/4 to 1/2 cup of white vinegar to the water before boiling the jars.

Adding white vinegar to the water prevents the buildup of this white film and helps keep your jars looking their best.

Step 3: Inspect jars for defects: one of the most critical steps in preparing jars for canning is to inspect each one. Discard those that have scratches, cracks, or an uneven rim.

You can toss the damaged ones in the bin or set them aside for dry storage or craft projects. Even if your jars are brand new, don't skip this essential step.

Step 4: Wash them with soapy water: Wash brand-new jars in hot soapy water. You could wash them in the dishwasher instead of by hand. You don't need to be picky about cleaning jars unless they are super dirty. Just give them a quick wash.

Step 5: Rinse the jars clean: Rinse the jars thoroughly, taking care to remove all soap.

Since you will be putting them in boiling water, it is critical to rinse them in hot water and put them in the pot or canner right away.

While you are working to sterilize the canning jars, never let the glass cool before putting them in hot water, or they may break.

I like to fill the jars before adding them to the pot. That way, I don't have to fill the pot so full in Step 1 and take that heavy thing to the stove.

Step 6: Put the hot jars in the canner: Gently add the hot, clean jars to the water in the canner, placing them upright.

Do not drop them into the water or let them bang against each other. This may cause them to break or splinter.

Also, if you carelessly put them in the canner, it will splash boiling water everywhere. Ouch.

To avoid this, turn the empty jars sideways as you slowly dip them into the water. A jar lifter is essential for moving them in and out of boiling water.

You could use regular kitchen tongs for this, but they're a little clunky and don't hold as well as a mason jar lifter.

Step 7: Cover every jar with water: Once all the jars are cleaned and placed in the hot bath container, add more water to cover them (if needed) completely.

Step 8: Boil all the jars: Bring the water to a boil and keep it with the jars fully submerged for 10 minutes to sterilize them.

You can turn off the stove once they are done boiling, but do not remove the jars from the canner until you are ready to fill them.

If you let them cool, they may break as you fill them with hot liquid or when you process them. Also, even cold jars will not form a proper seal once the lids are applied.

Frequently asked questions

Preparing mason jars for canning is simple, but you may have some questions. Below are some of the most common answers I get about sterilizing jars.

Do you need to sterilize jars?

No, it is not always necessary to sterilize the jars before use.

You can skip this step if you process them in a pressure cooker after filling or if the instructions in your recipe say you don't need to sterilize the jars first.

This extra step doesn't hurt, however. And it will keep your jars clean, safe, and ready no matter what food storage method you use.

Will a glass jar break in boiling water?

It will probably break if you put a cold glass jar in hot water. That is why heating the glass is essential before boiling it in water.

You can warm them first by running them under lukewarm water and raising them slowly until they are hot. Or remove the jars from the dishwasher while they are still hot.

Do you need to sterilize pickling jars?

Yes, I recommend sterilizing the jars before pickling unless your recipe says it is unnecessary. Always follow the exact instructions in the recipe for safety.

Can you sterilize jars in the oven?

No. Using the oven isn't an effective way to sterilize jars. The only safe way to do this is to boil them in hot water for at least 10 minutes, as described above.

Preparing jars for canning is easy and doesn't take much time. Once you are familiar with the process, there is nothing to do. And proper sterilization of jars will ensure that your food is healthy and safe.

Food supplies for evacuation

If you are traveling, you will need food.

Ready-to-eat meals are the military solution to food on the go and work for survival. These meals have everything you need to stay on the move inside, complete with a flameless heating element.

Although expensive and sometimes cumbersome, you are packing three to six in a large prepper bag is a good choice. You can also easily store a full box inside a vehicle designed for emergencies, giving you a ready supply of food on the road.

Besides that, dehydrated foods are excellent. Adding water gives you a meal, and they take up almost no space.

High-calorie, protein-rich foods such as crackers and peanut butter are also very helpful in giving you energy when needed.

Sugar is generally bad, while carbohydrates and proteins are energy foods.

Conservation

Food preservation is a simple matter.

Decades of food preparation in and out of the home have given many people enough ideas to take on the road, and you may already have some at home. All you have to do is make sure the food is safe.

All food storage should be airtight and watertight. This will help it last longer and help you avoid spoiling food while on the go.

Complex cases offer more protection but can be bulkier. Simple food-sealing bags are probably the best solution on the go. Your food might get crushed, but it won't take up much space in your bag.

Preparation

As for preparation, the best thing is easy. Stick with foods that can be eaten cold, if possible, but that requires nothing more than a fire to cook are best.

You may or may not have access to an oven or stovetop where you are going, so try to stick to something simple.

Good preparation should involve a campfire, a flameless heating element, or some sort of simple rehydration.

You may not have time to cook as you move, so anything that can be eaten directly from a wrap is useful. That said, never eat anything that should be cooked without fully cooking it: burned is better than cooked, as it will make illness much less likely.

Kitchen kit

You are lucky if you can fit a cooking kit in your car or carry a bag. That will increase the safety of your food, give you more cooking options, and may even provide you with a heat source.

Many fantastic camp stoves are available, but the real goal should be to look for size and efficiency. Ideally, a small one-burner camp stove, preferably gas or solar, is ideal.

All you need to cook is one small pot and one small pan, allowing you to prepare almost anything.

A good kit will include all of these items and the essential tools and should come with a cup. That will last longer than you think if you save fuel and treat the tools respectfully.

PART 4: THE PREPPER'S HOME DEFENSE

Your home is the very definition of comfort. It is often best to stay where you are in a disaster situation.

It is often said, "there is no place like home." It is a cliché that certainly rings true for those facing the aftermath of a disaster. The home provides the very definition of comfort.

The home will become less peaceful when a family is without power. There may be structural damage. A house is not so welcoming when part of the roof collapses under the weight of a fallen tree. The yard may become a nest of tangled branches and downed utility lines.

Your home is an excellent headquarters for recovery in an emergency. You should build your emergency plans with the home in mind.

The work to be done might be daunting, but it is still the most familiar place in the family. It is a common point that binds the family together. It provides an advantage that cannot be overstated amidst the inevitable stress caused by the catastrophe.

The house is an excellent venue for recovery in an efficient sense. It is the place where equipment is stored. An organized prepper could take a flashlight, enter the dark workshop and find the precise tool needed for any job. You should build most of your projects with the home in mind.

Families who have made proper preparation will have meals stashed in food cupboards to keep everyone well fed for a good duration/length of time. Those who have assembled the right tools and supplies should have the ability to stay warm and dry and have plenty to drink while the community at large slowly heals from its bruises.

Our homes are our castles. You might ask why a family would ever evacuate. The answer is clear and straightforward. A prepper should not focus his main concerns on the days or weeks when nature has shown its power. He should worry primarily about the disaster itself.

Safety is the first objective, so it makes the most sense to move away from imminent danger if it is reasonably possible. Preppers should pay close attention to incoming hazard warnings and make quick, reasoned decisions. Often, signs are insufficient and leave you with no choice but to stay in place and use all the tools and supplies you have stashed away.

The key is to make an intelligent, unemotional decision. It is easy to imagine a prepper becoming stubborn and taking a firm stance, particularly with all the time and money spent keeping track of food, water, and tools. Someone who has spent a good chunk of salary on a generator and accumulated a good supply of gas might realize it is time to put it to use. A person with this mindset misses the point of preparation. A plan is not about things. Instead, it is all that stuff that supports the project.

The most significant point of preparation is to exercise the foresight necessary to make it through everything the world puts in your way and by the best possible means. Home is comfort. Security, however, should always trump ease and abundance. Imagine all the second guesses that would come if a family member suffered a significant injury due to a weather event.

Home is sometimes the safest place to be. Very often, there is no reasonable way to avoid danger. The decision to huddle in the safe room in the basement is usually made by Mother Nature when events such as tornadoes or even severe thunderstorms that bring tremendous straight-line winds strike quickly.

Mother Nature can get ugly pretty quickly.

Survival is the primary goal, but comfort can be achieved after laying the groundwork for preparedness. A good plan would include various elements beyond the rule of three. Further efforts would focus on how to keep life as normal as possible during periods of upheaval.

Comfort means lighting. It could include a method of cooking. If you have children at home, it would be wise to have any number of diversions to keep children's minds occupied if they miss computers, TV, and video games.

Planning is not a process aimed at making a recovery easy. No amount of preparation could offer that kind of guarantee. However, those who plan thoughtfully and thoroughly are taking steps that would make the consequences of a disaster much more manageable. A well-prepared family would be better equipped to deal with their problems briskly.

Destructive events would be difficult to some extent for anyone. Even those managing recovery from the comfort of home would see their patience wither. A preparer might find a silver lining in knowing that the recovery mechanisms in place today are far greater than those available to struggling communities in decades past.

Modern technology, with all its more problematic impacts, has also made life safer and recovery efforts much more efficient.

Building a small underground storage/storm shelter is a reasonable way to keep your survival or recovery supplies safe as long as you are in an area that does not flood.

After disasters, the capacity for growth did not outweigh the benefits of proper planning. Assistance provided to the masses could never account for the unique considerations of any individual. With the help of a preparedness plan, your property would inevitably give greater comfort and a most critical level of privacy that you will not find in a large-scale community shelter.

Preparation goes beyond the environment. Having a kitchen, a living room, and only a few small bedrooms would not seem like much for the young family in a starter home living in typical calm. However, you would gain much greater appreciation if you were forced to occupy a small place among hundreds of unfolded cribs in a makeshift shelter such as large gyms or shopping malls. Food on hand is better for your spirit, confidence, and sense of normalcy than standing in line for whatever meal is served by aid workers that day.

Safety comes first. Inevitable hazards in any region should give families a particular reason to consider all available means to prevent harm. Some components of preparedness take into account the very moments of danger.

Prepare the food. Conserve some water. Learn how to collect water and make it drinkable.

Preparing the home through preparation beyond the basics requires a variety of thoughts and decisions. Solutions would differ from prepper to prepper. Several methods are available to achieve the many goals of a prepper. The rule of three is the beginning.

If you have a generator as part of your plan, make sure you have enough gas on hand to make it worthwhile if an emergency occurs for some days. It is difficult to predict what amounts would be sufficient. You might consider emptying the gas canisters in the car after some time. The gas goes bad after a while. You should recognize that factor and figure out how to consider it as part of your planning.

For reasons of preparedness, environmentalism, or both, some households would forgo the gas generator and rely on a different way to secure electricity. Some might install solar panels or build wind turbines. These are expensive in terms of initial investment but offer the possibility of recoupment (plus, there are tax deductions). Often, such systems will allow people to take their furnace, water heater, or other expensive necessities off the grid and, by proxy, off their electric bill.

Families should prepare somehow for the possibility of criminal activity in the aftermath of any disastrous event. In this sense and many others, one element of preparation is maintaining a good relationship with one's neighbor. Everyone needs allies. It makes sense to have those closest to you on your side.

Often, the best protection you can have for your home is the watchful eyes of the people around you.

That is an area of preparation that may not have been considered years ago. It would have been standard practice. But people seem to be becoming more and more isolated. Many people today do not take the time to get to know their neighbors as people did years ago.

It is worth meeting, chatting, and having a barbecue during the summer.

Planning for a robust home recovery requires a range of thoughts extending beyond its four walls' confines. It takes a lot of excellent and honest thinking. It takes a combination of enormous efforts and many smaller tasks to make a disaster of any size more bearable for your family.

Bitter cold can be hazardous in a disaster situation.

Those during an emergency would like to keep a specific number at the top of their minds. There is no more important figure for human life than 36°C. It is the standard, healthy temperature of the human body. Biology does not allow you to waver much on either side of that marker for long without incurring some terrible consequences.

The potential for problems is not limited to extreme temperatures. High heat brings as much, if not more, danger than bitter cold. Various factors could play a role in shifting body temperature out of balance. Alcohol, for example, can lower body temperature despite its tendency to warm a person. Some medications raise body temperature and could put you at risk if summer temperatures rise beyond what is bearable.

Life requires a rather delicate balance. Anyone could quickly fall into serious trouble by moving above or below 36°C by even a few degrees. It is essential to have a way to correct it.

Body temperature represents the most crucial and fundamental survival factor. It is a piece of preparation that requires the utmost attention, although it is not always seen as a factor of concern. Many would more quickly think of food or water as more significant issues when questioned about the critical needs of life. Without adequate shelter, you would not go far enough for those otherwise vital components to come into play.

For a trainer, the ability to account for body temperature provides the very meaning of shelter. Most think of shelter as a place to take refuge from the elements. That is an essential part of the big picture.

Preppers, however, go a step further and rely on the term to describe any method that allows you to keep your body temperature as close to normal as possible. A shelter could be a shade tree or a cold water bottle for those who begin to feel tired when caught outdoors in high humidity under a blazing sun. The shelter could be a parka, hat, and gloves for those stuck during unbearably cold temperatures.

Small things sometimes make a big difference. The trainer would recognize a shelter in something as simple as a silicone sheet. It could be the clothes on your back. The shelter could be the small box of waterproof matches in your front pocket if you need to start a fire. The critical point at any time, place, or situation is to stick strictly to 36 degrees. Life depends on it.

A family could often better meet its needs from home with the right contingencies. Those who live in cold-weather areas might recognize that the gas or electric oven is a great tool, but they are not foolproof. Preparation will take into account the loss of the furnace. Those who live in areas prone to extreme heat might think about how they would fare without the central air conditioner. Those lost or stuck have different problems to work on to maintain that essential balance.

The high level of danger posed by the lack of adequate shelter should promptly draw the focused attention of a trainer. Those pushed far enough away from their average body temperature have only three hours to cool down or warm up, depending on their situation. If 36 degrees is the most important number for your well-being, a related figure provided by the rule of three follows very closely.

It is a frightening number. Three hours is often a pretty tight deadline, even for many of the insignificant affairs in daily life. The rule of three tells us that a short period is all that would separate life and death without a way to warm or cool your body. The clock starts ticking as soon as your body temperature shifts sufficiently from the norm. Those in survival mode have no time to waste.

The cold side of the equation is medically referred to as hypothermia. A person reaches that condition when the internal body temperature drops to 35°C degrees or less. It is amazing how much just 1°C degree means to our well-being.

Those who do not know the warning signs could face enormous risks when symptoms begin to manifest. Symptoms often occur pretty gradually, and someone suffering might not even recognize something is wrong. That is quite a dangerous state of affairs when considered from the rule of three, but even more so because it is a risk that could creep in for those who have not thought adequately about the future.

In addition, the very nature of the symptoms can add another level of concern as hypothermia progresses. Its toll on the body has a way of masking the danger. Too few of those who live in cold climate areas, for example, tend to think so much about shivering.

Many people may attest that they did not make the best decisions about their well-being while intoxicated. That is not so different. Those suffering from hypothermia often experience confusion and disorientation as the condition worsens.

The point could come during hypothermia, where you would lack the mental means to recognize or understand the severity of what is happening to your body. It could go far beyond your ability to realize that you just need some warmth. Those in pain would eventually lose consciousness if they did not have the means to raise their body temperature. At that point, you would be very close to death.

It is a condition that further illustrates why it is critical to know and understand all the significant risks you might face in a survival situation or the aftermath of a disaster. Hypothermia is more likely to occur in colder temperatures, although not necessarily. Many people would not consider the possibility of dying from lack of heat in probably comfortable temperatures. It is, however, a threat in temperatures of 40°C degrees or more.

Wood stoves provide a lot of heat, require no electricity, and give you a place to cook and heat water for bathing.

Hyperthermia, on the other hand, becomes a concern when the body temperature moves to more than 38 degrees. Many of those suffering from the condition have problems with dehydration in combination with their dangerously high body temperature.

Severe cases on the high side of thermal imbalance could also confuse those suffering. People suffering from hyperthermia would lose consciousness and die rapidly due to the lack of some means of cooling down slowly and steadily. As the condition persists, blood pressure would fall. Organs would eventually collapse.

Those who know and respect the risks and symptoms have already made great strides. For example, those who are cold, shivering, and notice a bit of clumsiness should be aware of making heat their only priority. Those walking around between that brutally hot mid- to late-summer temperatures and experiencing nausea, headaches, and dizziness should recognize that it is time to get into an air-conditioned room or anywhere colder without delay.

Surviving the elements

Good shelter planning could begin outside of any concern for disaster. It should be thought out from the standpoint of basic survival. Those leaving home should think about the possibility of an emergency and have some supplies to keep warm or cool with them. Always think "three hours." Ideas and the flexibility to improvise may sometimes make up for what you lack in gear.

It starts with communication. We live in an age where you cannot escape the barrage of messages. They come from those we know, those we don't know, and whether they are wanted or not. Interestingly, communication is still so often forgotten.

We have all heard of the boy who cries wolf. There is a good reason why the story has retained its enduring power. Hunters, fishermen, bikers, hikers, or anyone else heading beyond the expanses of civilization should never forget to let someone, in general, know where they are running and the time they intend to return. When plans go awry, your best bet for first aid is always to leave with a friend or loved one before going out on the trail or in the field. Make sure someone knows when to send out a search party. Make sure friends or family can take it seriously.

Meeting the body's need for a balanced temperature could be done through the contents of a travel bag.

Those with a healthy respect for the rule of three would not travel far beyond home without having their bags handy. A good suitcase would represent shelter in several ways.

There is a shawl that I could quickly grab if the clouds decided to open up and make life much harder. The contents of the bag include a change of warm, dry clothing. There is a tarp tucked inside, and I have a small tent to provide shelter from any potentially problematic elements, whether cold winds, rain, or hot sun.

A travel bag helps make life easier, but this assumes that you have thought out your entire plan and diligently grabbed your gear before venturing out. All of us growing up probably had the imagination to build different forts in many different ways. Those trapped in the elements without an assortment of supplies may have to return to some childhood creativity.

The unprepared person who recognizes that he or she is stuck and may be out there for a while could quickly gather sticks and twigs and set up a canopy to stay dry if it starts to rain. Those caught in winter could buy some time and increase their chances with a snow shelter. A couple caught in the rain with a poncho in between could stretch it out and slide it between some branches to create an improvised roof. Desperate times call for the use of a bit of creativity.

Preparing for and overcoming a cold weather emergency and staying in place should begin with recognizing that gas and electricity connections have not always existed. People throughout history have weathered the worst weather that nature could bring. Those of us living today can do the same, but we might do it better by imagining the misery of being overcome unprepared.

The furnace is a beautiful and often reliable appliance, but it is still too often taken for granted. Those who live in climates with subzero temperatures for nearly half the calendar year might reevaluate relying on one to provide adequate heat and safety. It may not be a matter of disaster. Cars fall into disrepair. The one big snowstorm that knocks out the substation might just as quickly remind households of the need for a backup plan.

Those people should take the initiative and consider their options before any winter event cuts off gas or electricity. A boxer would not require a punch in the face to know the wisdom of putting himself or herself on guard. Many arrangements families might make to keep their families safe in such circumstances are sensible and for reasons beyond the scope of preparedness. Winter can be a drain on the wallet. It is less so for homes that have been correctly assembled to account for the cold.

Ensuring the house has a reasonable degree of insulation would keep heat inside and cold beyond the walls. Every degree would be necessary if a family lost its furnace in its time of need. It is a project that aims to save a family some money even during the calmer winters. The stove does not have to work so hard if the house does not give up all the heat it produces so quickly.

Unfortunately, fireplaces are included less often in newly built homes. They provide a great source of heat and a cozy gathering place for the family. A fireplace could become an option for some living in homes without one. Many, however, may find themselves limited by finances or lack of a good wall to accommodate one.

Wood stoves would also require effort and investment, but they are often much more feasible than the traditional fireplace. They are functional. A furnace would provide a lot of heat to a house, whether during a break or otherwise. It is a matter of heat before furnishings.

Many people have invested in the latest pellet stoves. They burn compressed wood. They do this efficiently and without too much trouble or effort. Models are available that would open the option even to those with smaller homes. You can buy a window-mount model that is no different in size than the air conditioners that many people have. These options would require some upfront expense but save the family some money in the long run. If used regularly, traditional wood stoves and pellet stoves of any kind would lighten some of the heating load on the furnace.

Those who are not in the right place to make a significant initial investment in an excellent secondary heat source could still assemble smaller, less expensive options to provide some heat if Mother Nature puts the family in a difficult situation.

Earlier I mentioned oil lamps as a contingency that I like in terms of function and decor. It is an instrument that goes back more than a century. It played an essential role in the era just before electricity became commonplace in the average home.

The technology may be antiquated compared to all our modern marvels. Still, there is little better to have in the home when the electricity fails, and a family is stuck with the capabilities their ancestors had more than 100 years ago. It is an excellent source of light. One lamp would provide 60 watts of light, enough to see how to move around safely and adequate reading light. For preppers, it gives much more; one lamp offers 2,200 BTUs of heat; that's enough heat to take the chill out of a 10-by-10 room.

Oil lamps are still manufactured and available on the market. Antique versions are bound to look better and probably cost less. You might also keep an eye on flea markets, second-hand stores, or Internet e-commerce. The lamp that is a century old will still work and offer the same functionality as the new model just unpacked from its box. Any family would do well to have several in the house to account for light and a means of raising the temperature.

Those who stayed in the cold, prepared or not, should not panic regardless of how brutal the temperatures outside became. The home might lose some comfort, but it would remain a valuable refuge from the cold weather outside. Those without the right tools would have a more challenging time, but it would take time before survival became an issue.

One of the essential considerations in a cold weather emergency would go beyond comfort and safety issues. The temperature of a home would drop but at a relatively slow rate. If you do not have a backup heat source, you would want to take steps to ensure that pipes do not burst. If the cold persists, you want to shut off the water and drain what was left inside. It would often take weeks of pretty miserable temperatures to reach that point.

Families should make the best of what they have in a cold weather emergency. The sun is an excellent source of warmth. Opening up the shadows would allow the sun to provide some warmth. Often it is enough to raise the house's temperature by a few degrees.

Those who live in colder climate zones would have some contingencies ready, regardless of whether they are preppers. Everyone would be bound to have long underwear, a good supply of heavy sweatshirts, and warm blankets on hand. That would be enough for survival, if not for comfort.

Those struggling with cold weather should keep in mind some primary safety considerations. Coal is a vast and cheap heat source common to most households, although it should never be burned inside the home. The risk of carbon monoxide poisoning would put the family at much greater risk than any temperature, no matter how uncomfortable they feel. Carbon monoxide poisoning could kill within minutes. Those entirely defenseless to the temperature would die within three hours. Generators should never be used in the home for the same reason.

Those who live in cold climates would like to extend shelter planning to their cars. Many of us spend good periods of our days on the road. Of course, any good prepper would have their own bag in the back seat. There are, however, many other tools you would like to have stored in the trunk that could reduce the chances of shelter becoming a problem. Those who drive in snow or ice always run a reasonable risk of going off the road. Those who operate in rural areas may run the risk of getting stuck there for some time.

Motorists should keep a snow shovel in the trunk. You could put it under and around the tires to provide some traction. Road salt, sand, or cat litter is a vital package to take away. Sometimes, these tools are not enough.

Recognizing the importance of self-reliance, you should keep a set of jumper ropes and a tow chain in the trunk. You should have road signs to serve as beacons for others. You cannot guarantee that any Good Samaritan who stops by will have the right tools for the job. It is always a blessing to see someone ready and willing to help in a difficult situation.

A prepper should make good use of space. The biggest challenge of a travel bag is putting together a package that is light, compact, and meets the rule of three. The bag probably would not hold a sleeping bag. The trunk or back seat of any vehicle certainly would. You could survive on less, but you can never underestimate the power of a minimum of comfort during a difficult situation.

Preppers who anticipate challenges can often avoid them. A good prepper should always keep the gas tank full, whether hot or cold. Those with a lower degree of vigilance who drive in winter should know that they are setting themselves up for big trouble by letting the gas tank drop below half complete. The car or truck will not move if the fuel lines are frozen.

Plan, prepare, and practice.

If you haven't already figured it out, preparation is one of the most significant needs for those who want to keep a prepper bag.

You can't just throw these items in a bag and hope for the best you need a plan, and you need to make sure you update it as frequently as possible.

A prepper bag is not a lifelong supply of supplies. It is something you need to survive until you find a more sustainable situation.

Your first question is always where you want to go. You can't wander in the woods for the rest of your life, and you can't hope to survive on the contents of a backpack. Walking around with a prepper bag and no destination is a great way to die.

Once you know where you want to go, you must figure out how to get there. Do you know the terrain? Can you drive or ride a bike, or will you have to walk?

That will not only let you know what kind of bag you need but how long you will need to be on the move.

If you can figure it out, you can pack adequate food and water for your trip. If you don't know how to get to your safe place, you could be in serious trouble.

BOB and transportation

You have to take time to figure out where you're going, of course, but getting there is an entirely different problem. Unless you have a pilot's license, you will have three transportation options in an emergency: road, water, or walking.

You cannot depend on public transportation in an emergency and certainly do not want to hitchhike. As such, your means of transport is essential. A car gives you temporary shelter, additional storage space, and a quick way to reduce travel time.

Unfortunately, a situation that requires the elimination of bugs could clog highways and take cars out of the equation, as well as the danger of radiation.

One only has to look at recent disasters to see how quickly the gas supply can be used up in a populated region, and roads can become disaster areas even if things are still going well.

A motorcycle is usually better if you are alone, but carrying a lot on a bike can be difficult. Bicycles are an option, but only if you can go off-road with your bag.

Water transportation is a good choice, but only if you own a boat.

Nothing beats a boat if you're going to an island or somewhere across a lake. Even a small boat can triple your storage space, while larger vessels can provide you with a place to shelter and live if things get particularly tough.

Your real enemy on the water is your skill level: unless you are skilled at driving a boat, you might as well stay away. There are dozens of hazards on the water, and most can kill you more efficiently than any disaster.

Your best means of transportation is still your feet.

Do some hiking, get good boots, and hope for the best. Use other transportation when you need it, but be prepared to walk.

The shelter

The shelter is the place you escape to during a disaster.

It can be anything from a short-term shelter to where you begin the process of starting over, but it should always be a place where you can refuel, rest, and plan. Therefore, you should take time to consider the location of your shelter.

Your first consideration should be ease of access. It should be far enough from regular traffic where only you know its location but close enough that you can access it in an emergency.

Take a moment to consider your transportation options before planning: if you have a boat, a remote island might work. If not, it should be a place where you can walk or drive in a few days.

It can be anything from a well-stocked tree house to a small cabin, but it has to be something that only you can access.

Once you have placed the shelter, you should ensure it is stocked with valuable items. It is helpful if it is stocked with twice as much food and water as you can carry in your backpack and twice as much of anything in your prepper bag.

If you can do this, you will have created a sanctuary for yourself to plan your future moves.

BOB practice makes perfect

The prepper bag is not something you can do at the last minute.

Many would-be survivors have fantasies of putting together a lot of food and ammunition and living the life of a wanderer. Still, the reality of the situation is that you have to practice the hunting process.

Take time to ensure you know where each item you need for your bag is; they should all stay in the bag. If not, practice packing.

Do this at night and during the day, and preferably try to interrupt your sleep cycle for the process. After doing this, take some time to practice with the bag.

Load it with as much weight as the bag can bear and take it on a long walk. Make sure you can walk several miles daily without the bag causing you pain.

If you have the ability, you may also want to take some time to try living with the bag.

A two- or three-day camping trip is a great way to practice your survival skills and should tell you what you forgot.

This safe practice is an excellent way to figure out what is needed and what is not in your bag without endangering your survival.

The more you practice this way, the more comfortable you will feel and the more ready you will be if and when you need to go out.

Miscellaneous preparations

Papers

Papers have a rather strange place in the world of survival.

Although they are simple pieces of paper worth very little during a disaster, they are perhaps the most important things to save from your home when you hit the road.

If you have to leave, you should always keep the possibility of returning home open. As such, there are certain documents you must always carry.

It is worth carrying your ID card with you. It is one of the few documents that show who you are, and it is challenging to get a duplicate in a disaster situation.

You should also take the time to carry other similar essential documents such as a passport or driver's license.

If you own a house, any document showing that you own the property is a must: things get confusing after a disaster, and you may be forced to prove that you own the property.

In addition to this, you should keep documents related to your business or other pieces of property or bank accounts with you (don't just keep them saved on your computer, this tool will be short-lived).

If it can help you restore your life after things are back to normal, it's probably worth taking.

Always remember to make copies and remember to carry originals with you at all times. They are more valuable in court and can help you reestablish claims if something goes wrong.

Identification

Your ID is one of the most important things you can bring. It can show who you are, give you access to specific resources in an emergency, and help you restore your life when and if things calm down again.

Your driver's license should always be in your wallet, so this should not be a problem. Be sure to carry other forms of photo identification, especially if they give you access to any resources.

That means memberships in professional organizations or even a gym membership-you never know where you might have to go when the going gets tough.

Money

If you think of taking money with you, you need to remember two things.

First, remember that cash is king if things go wrong. A few hundred in gold or silver will give you more than you can imagine and will be helpful for a long time, but remember not to become a target. Never carry only a debit or credit card; stay only with cash or gold/silver coins.

Second, remember that cash goes a long way in a disaster. If you are trying to survive something important, it is much better to bring something you can barter with, such as medication, food, or alcohol, but remember that these items can be bulky.

Cash is only valid as long as people continue to assign value to it.

Tools

Tools are what separate humans from animals.

If you are evacuating, you must take some tools with you. Unfortunately, you will not be able to take the entire toolbox with you.

However, you can fit some of your most essential tools in a prepper bag without much space.

A multi-tool will still be your best friend, but bring two screwdrivers and a simple wrench.

A carpenter's hammer is also a necessity: it can serve multiple purposes.

If you have a set of jeweler's screwdrivers at home, take them-they to weigh only a few ounces, but they can be invaluable for repairing your equipment.

The BOB (Bug-Out-Bag) checklist

You can easily find most of these items on Amazon, but you should research and evaluate each item/equipment according to your specific needs before purchasing.

Prepper bag

CFP90/Mil-Tec style backpack.

Military-style duffle bag (as a vehicle bag).

Backpack/waterproof duffel/zip-lined bag.

Also, consider ready-made evacuation kits or disaster survival kits available on Amazon.

Water

Collapsible water bottles - various sizes.

Stainless steel cup

Water purification tablets.

Water filtration system.

Moisturizing pack

Also, consider powdered drinks and electrolyte compounds.

Food

Ready-to-eat meals are best kept in insect pouches and include dry and/or dehydrated meals.

Walnuts and chocolate

Protein bars/candy.

Dried or canned fruits.

Dried and canned meats/vegetables (pay attention to water content in cans because they increase in weight).

Crackers/biscuits

Peanut butter, jams, and spreads.

Tea and coffee

Soup packets.

Cheese and dried eggs.

Dry or canned milk (can be used for infants/children).

Salt and pepper

Set of utensils (fork, spoon).

Can opener

Make sure you put together enough calories to take home plus 25 percent more. Also, consider energy gel packs.

Garments

Thermal underwear

Hiking socks (wool and cotton).

Hiking boots and running shoes.

Pants - running and rain pair.

Breathable t-shirts.

Heavy cotton t-shirts for UV protection.

Long-sleeved shirts

Lightweight fleece/sweater.

Jacket or hoodie.

Leather gloves - heavy duty, weather-specific pair.

Brim hat - weather-specific.

Scarf and balaclava

Rainwear: waterproof jacket and pants.

Ponchos that double as shelter.

<u>Remember, you will need a change of clothes for yourself and your family.</u>

Shelter and bedding

Lightweight tent - 4 seasons

Sheet/sheet or ground pad

Sleeping bag and sack liner

Emergency blanket/space

Wool blankets

Plastic or polyester cloth

Rope, twine, and tape

Carabiners and spare pegs

Poncho lining

Sanitation and hygiene

Disinfectant and wet wipes for children.

Toilet paper and tissues.

Hand sanitizer

Lightweight towels.

Compact toothbrush and toothpaste.

Dental Floss

Mouthwash

Soap and shower gel.

Deodorant

Small mirror

Nail clippers

Razors and shaving foam/oil.

Collapsible basin

Plastic comb

Heavy waste bags

Foldable survival camping shovel with pick

First aid and medicines

A small and compact first aid book.

Good first-aid kit with sterile dressings, sterile gauze, bandages, band-aids, alcohol-soaked wipes/pads, medical tape, antiseptic, antifungal and antibiotic creams, sutures, butterfly fasteners, etc.

Pair of tweezers, scissors, and magnifying glass.

Latex gloves

Hydrogen peroxide and Betadine.

Scalpel blades and handles.

Emergency dental repair kit

Insect repellent

Safety pins

Sunscreen

Lip balm

Eyewash

Vitamins

Thermometer

Finger splints

Months of over-the-counter medications for Pain relief, diarrhea, vomiting, allergies, constipation, bloating, decongestant, etc.

Copies of any prescriptions

All group members should have a complete copy of their medical records with emergency contact numbers and names. Always seek medical advice when planning medications.

Communications and navigation

Mobile phone with helpful apps.

GPS with your home marked.

Compass with illumination

Waterproof mini-binoculars

Maps of your shelter and facilities such as hospitals, etc.

Waterproof bags for phones and maps.

Spare batteries

Solar power chargers and adapters.

Hand crank loader

Emergency radio with crank handle

Small notepad and pencil

Emergency whistle

Note: Even if your cell phone network goes down, you may find it helpful to have apps on your phone for compass, flashlight level, etc.

Lighting and heat

Multi-fuel stove with extra fuel

Waterproof matches and windproof lighter.

Tinder

Metal fuel bottles.

Cookware set

Metal pot

Metal cup

Fork and spoon

Pot scrubber

Candles

LED headlamp

Glow sticks

LED keychain light

Hand-cranked flashlight

Headlamp with extra batteries

Self-defense and weapons

Folding knife

Rifle with hunting scope.

Ammunition

Pepper spray

Assault harness

Weapons cleaning kit.

Pocket knife: locks the blade.

Fixed-blade knife with sheath.

Sharpening stone (in the pocket on the sheath).

Hunting/survival knife with fire starter.

Aluminum crossbow and arrows.

Foldable survival camping shovel with pick

Emergency whistle

ID card, documents, and money

Identification documents: passport, driver's license, etc.

Medication and immunization registry.

Ownership documents: stocks, deeds, etc.

Marriage/birth certificates

Wallet with 500- 1000 dollars in small bills.

Mixed objects

Cotton bandana

Adhesive tape

Reclosable bags of different sizes.

Sunglasses

Sewing repair kit with buttons and nylon thread.

Polyethylene pipe for siphoning.

Fishing kit

Waterproofing enamel for boots

Repair kit

Pack assorted needles

Bible or other inspirational material.

Deck of cards

An extra pair of glasses.

Multi-tool and screwdrivers

Hand saw or pull saw.

Multi-purpose ax or folding spade and pickaxe.

Pets

Collapsible water bowl.

Food and water for 72 hours.

Certificate of vaccination

Leash and muzzle

This list isn't conclusive, but it should give you an idea of the essential items to pack.

It should be reviewed and updated regularly to allow for substitution of perishable content, such as food, and specific customization according to circumstances and evolving knowledge of preparation.

I hope you continue to plan and prepare for all eventualities, and I wish you well in your preparations.

You can construct shelters to provide excellent protection against all effects of nuclear weapons except in places in cratered areas. Most shelters would be of little use in areas prone to high fallout unless sufficient life-support equipment allows occupants to remain in the shelters until outside conditions become bearable. But In regions at increased risk of relapse, most high protection factor shelters would be crowded. Except in the cold season, most would need a ventilation pump to remove heated air and bring in outside air cool enough to maintain optimal temperature-humidity conditions. The means to store adequate water is another essential requirement for life support.

Basement shelters

A massive all-out attack's explosion and fire effects would destroy or damage most houses and other buildings and endanger the occupants of shelters within them. Outside of explosive areas and/or fires, the use of shelters inside buildings would not be as dangerous. However, an enemy could also target some areas where large numbers of people had been evacuated before the attack, although it is believed that such targeting is not included in an enemy strategy.

Appropriate earth-covered shelters in an explosive area offer better protection against injury from explosion, fire, or fallout than almost any basement. But during the most likely types of crises that threaten nuclear war, most citizens, including those who will evacuate to areas outside likely blast zones, would probably lack the tools, materials, space, determination, physical strength, or time to build good shelters. As a result, without better protection, most unprepared urbanites would have to use the basements and other shelters of existing structures. Shelters in buildings, including basement shelters, have the same requirements as useful shelters: adequate shielding against fallout radiation, resistance, adequate ventilation, cooling, water, fallout radiation meters, food, hygiene, etc...

Public shelters

In unexpected attacks, many unprepared people must evacuate to nearby designated public shelters. Public shelters can save millions of lives in densely populated areas hit by explosions, fires, and heavy rains.

All people concerned about survival should remember that most officially inspected and marked shelters offer better radiation protection than most unimproved domestic basements.

People preparing to go to public shelters should be aware that many lacks forced ventilation and that fans in most forced ventilation systems would be stopped by loss of electrical power due to electromagnetic pulse effects or other effects of nuclear explosions on electrical systems. A shock wave at an overpressure range of just 1 psi (65 pounds per square cm) would destroy most shelter ventilation fans. A person bringing 10 sizeable plastic garbage bags and 10 pillowcases to a public shelter to make 10 helpful water bags in which 60 liters of water could be stored would help himself and dozens of other occupants.

Self-defense and weapons

Weapons are not just tools: they can be a terrible liability.

A weapon is a source of protection, trust, and food in the right hands.

They can pose a greater danger to yourself and those you love in the wrong hands.

As a survival preparedness enthusiast, you must ensure you are responsible and prepared with your weapon.

Preparation means making sure you know how to use your weapon. Nothing in the world is more dangerous than a gun in the hands of a person who does not know how to use it.

It doesn't matter if you have a pistol or a rifle; go to the range and learn how to shoot. You must be a good enough marksman to bring down a target without missing, as you may never get a second shot.

Along with accuracy, you need to work on maintenance. You should be able to quickly disassemble, clean, repair, and reassemble a weapon.

If you don't know how to do it, take classes: there are manuals for almost every weapon ever made and videos to show you exactly how to work with it.

Accountability is another story.

Responsibility means keeping weapons safe and locked up. You can keep ammunition in your prepper bag, but never keep a rifle inside: it may be nearby, but You should permanently hide it.

When traveling, never point a rifle at anything unless you intend to shoot it.

You should keep rifles and knives out of the hands who do not know how to use them and should be treated with the utmost respect. The more careful you are, the better prepared you will be.

Self-injury vs. self-defense

The main goal of a survivor should always be to avoid trouble.

The real problem in a survival situation is that you cannot always avoid a fight when trying to keep yourself safe. Your most important goal is to determine when you can avoid a conflict and when you must defend yourself.

This is how you determine the difference between self-defense and self-injury.

Self-harm is often mistaken for a defensive measure.

When you take an offensive position, you are looking for trouble. This means interacting with others in a way that is sure to provoke a fight, always trying to avoid compromise, and taking violence as the first option.

This is a spectacular way to kill yourself while trying to survive because the attack almost always requires you to give the advantage to the defender.

Not only will they have adrenaline on their side, but they may have any number of tricks up their sleeve or weapons you haven't considered.

Self-defense is what you do to protect yourself.

Always try to get out of a situation, even with one hand on your weapon. If it comes down to it, you are usually safer giving up something than fighting, but you are never sure about giving up everything you need to survive.

Always remember that your goal is to stop the fight when acting in self-defense. That can vary from taking down an opponent long enough to run to taking the ultimate solution, but your goal is to conserve as much energy as possible and end things immediately.

There is never any shame in running but only do it if it will not put you in a worse position than standing still and defending yourself.

Survival knives

The category of survival knives is more extensive than you might think. These knives are sold in most sporting goods stores and big-box stores.

Unfortunately, most knives sold as survival equipment are nothing more than expensive showpieces.

Your ideal knife will have a fixed blade, should be able to be sharpened by hand, and will be large enough to deal with dense foliage or other hazards on the trail.

As a rule, you should pack more than one knife. A knife is easy enough to keep on you while traveling, and an extra survival blade will not take up much space in your backpack.

Even the best knives can break, so it is common sense to have a spare. When you make your initial purchase, treat the blade like any other reasonable piece of equipment: buy extra and test it to its breaking point.

Once you know how far you can push the knife, you will know whether or not it is valuable enough to take up space.

Decide what kind of shelter to build or use

Public and other existing shelters

The advantages of the vast majority of existing public and other shelters such as basements, subways, or any place underground:

- Their immediate availability in many locations, without labor or need to provide materials and tools.
- The provision of fair to excellent fall protection is generally much better than what citizens have available in their homes.
- The ability for people unable to bring food or water to a public shelter to share some brought by more foresighted occupants.

Disadvantages of the majority of public and other existing homes available to the majority of people:

- Most of them are in the target areas
- Poor protection against explosion, fire, and carbon monoxide.
- Lack of water and means to conserve it, and lack of food supplies.
- No reliable air pump, essential in hot weather to provide adequate ventilation-cooling to maintain sustainable conditions in fully occupied shelters, primarily underground.
- Uncertainty about the availability of Geiger counters and occupants who know how to use them.
- No reliable lighting, toilets, or other life-support equipment, with few exceptions.
- The crowding of large numbers of people unrelated to each other. In horrific situations that can last for weeks, the higher the number of people, the higher the risk of infections, hysteria epidemics, conflicts, and other conflicts. Proper underground shelters covered by earth.

Benefits of appropriate underground earth-covered fallout shelters:

- They offer good protection.
- Less time, labor, and materials are required to build them than to build equally protective above-ground projects.
- If built sufficiently separated from flammable houses and forests, they provide much better protection against fire hazards than shelters in buildings.
- When excavated in stable soil, even earth-walled types without props offer good explosion protection up to overpressure ranges of at least five psi, where an explosion or fire would destroy most houses and buildings.

Disadvantages of appropriate underground fallout shelters:

- Not practical where the water table or rocks are very close to the surface.
- It is not practical to build them on frozen ground.
- They are generally more crowded and uncomfortable than the best basement shelters.

Antiballistic shelters

Benefits of appropriate anti-explosion shelters (above 20,000 cost):

- Occupants of appropriate bomb shelters could survive unharmed in vast explosive areas where bomb shelters would not prevent death or injury.
- Explosion-proof doors protect occupants from shock waves, dangerous overpressure, wind gusts, and burns on exposed skin caused by the popcorn effect and heated air.
- The appropriate blast shelters were constructed and tested against explosions as part of explosive testing. The horizontal blast doors of these tested blast shelters were not damaged because they were protected on all sides by blast protection logs pointed together surrounded by earth ramps. Their air supply systems were not damaged by blast effects that would be bent or broken by the

above-ground vertical air supply pipes typical of even expensive imported Swiss and Finnish family permanent blast shelters.

Disadvantages of appropriate blast shelters:

- They require more time, materials, tools, skills, and labor than those needed to build bomb shelters.
- Particularly appropriate blast shelters should be well separated from buildings and forests, which, if burned, can produce dangerous amounts of carbon monoxide and toxic smoke.
- Their vents allow far more fallout particles to enter than the gooseneck vents and filters of typical permanent blast shelters. Fortunately, air blasts produce only tiny particles. Even though only a few are highly radioactive, they can easily be transported to earth in "hot spots" scattered by rain and snow. Thus relatively few immediate deaths or delayed cancer cases from air bursts are likely to occur.

WARNING:

Domestic fallout and anticlastic shelters must have PFs much higher than 40. In areas with high fallout, a significant proportion of PF 40 shelter residents are exposed to sufficient radiation doses to neutralize or kill them later.

In Italy, guidelines were updated in early March 2022 in case of a nuclear attack or danger of contamination from hazardous radiation spills from nuclear power plants located above and below 200 km away.

The warnings (most of them described above) include:

Sheltering indoors for 2-3 days.

Closing all windows and shutters.

Turn off air conditioning and all systems that take air from the outside.

I don't agree with these guidelines, as fallout particles can enter the house even if I try to isolate them as much as possible. If you do not have appropriate shelters, it is better to stay indoors rather than outdoors, but in the worst cases, you could still be exposed to a high dose of radiation.

PART 5: OFF-GRID LIVING

We all prepare in many ways, for many reasons, and for minor and significant needs. At the lower end of the scale, preparation is as irrelevant as looking in one's wallet before walking out the door to ensure a few dollars to pay for lunch. We prepare for the long term with investment plans to create a decent level of comfort when retirement age approaches.

Preparing for the most challenging times that any disaster could bring is not so common for the large population, but it still makes a lot of sense. No place on this vast planet is immune from the worst of Mother Nature. Today's efforts could provide your family with a fair degree of comfort even as the larger community struggles amid catastrophe. It takes some work and some thought. It is time and effort very well spent.

Teaching the means and methods of preparedness would be a much easier task if it required only a roundup of some basic strategies, a checklist of the tools needed, and some brief descriptions of how to use them. Many more people could take that critical path if a step-by-step plan could ensure that they would survive and thrive in a generic disaster situation. Of course, that is not how the world works.

A good preparedness plan for a family living in the country will differ from one for a family living in the city.

Preparation requires more than tools and supplies. It requires a proper mindset. It requires that you pay attention to the small complexities that fall within and contributes to the more significant potential problems that any family might face after a disaster. Different issues, meanwhile, require very different solutions.

An earthquake is not a tornado;

A fire is not a flood;

And a hurricane is not a blizzard;

No two disasters are identical.

Also, different people have different needs.

A few days without electricity would cause anyone some degree of discomfort. It would cause some people many more problems than others. The elderly man who needs an oxygen machine to live would face a much more critical situation even in a short-term power outage than the physically fit 32-year-old woman living in some houses down the street. We all have different circumstances.

Problems become much more significant for the unprepared as time passes. Supplies diminish. Patience runs out. Many families would indeed experience a substantial change in attitude and much greater trouble if a few days without electricity were extended to a few weeks.

Building a solid preparedness plan that considers survival and comfort after a disaster is a multifaceted task. Programs would differ from family to family, depending on how they live. Plans would also look very different based on where other families call home.

Risks, and thus contingencies, would vary by region.

A family's available space and resources would play to their efforts and abilities. A family on a property in the middle of a city will have less capacity than others to collect water and grow food. They would have to plan differently than the family living outside the city in a large country.

The risks differ in scope and likelihood depending on where you call home. Some might assess their threats and find comfort in a small-scale preparedness plan that would carry a family through a few weeks without having to meet needs beyond the home. Others might look at the odds and recognize a real potential for a significant catastrophe.

No preparedness guide could ever claim to provide detailed instructions applicable to anyone, in any place, or for any crisis. However, all people have the exact basic needs. Those skilled in planning rely on similar thoughts and principles to ensure well-being regardless of risk.

A good plan will require some tools. Any decent project will require stocking up in a way that most people today have not considered. Preparation goes deeper than the contents of the garage, pantry, and supply closet. It is a way of life.

Those who are best prepared continually work to develop knowledge and new skills that enable them to improvise and make the best use of what is at hand. Means of comfort and survival often come from purchased and stored items. In some cases, these means may come from the environment. The unpredictability is bound to become a factor when nature decides it is time to test your family. Preparation is always a work in progress.

There is, of course, the other side. Many people who have heard the term "prepper" probably have some degree of skepticism. They have probably drawn their ideas and some disturbing conclusions from news stories or programs about the small handful of people who live on the opposite end of the spectrum.

Indeed, some people have fully loaded shelters carrying food for several years. That group will generally keep a vast supply of tools and property well-protected. They are often heavily armed. They are working to find solutions should they be among the lone men and women left walking the planet.

The everyday family would do well to reject the unprepared and over-prepared ends of the scale. Most people would assess their comfort level after thinking about common, documented risks and finding good ways to handle difficult times somewhere in the vast middle ground.

Regarding preparation, you should not worry about the end of the world. Those who prepare for the future should recognize that all their supplies will run out. On the contrary, it is pretty smart to have the proper provisions for living comfortably outside your normal daily lifestyle. Those with no planning level are preparing their families to suffer far more than necessary when an emergency occurs. Those who have planned well beyond reasonable needs could probably have done better with their time, effort, and money. A level of preparedness that would sustain safety and comfort after the most typical and even most severe documented disasters would not resemble preparedness or lack thereof at either extreme.

The shelter requires immediacy when developing plans to overcome a disaster situation. If your house becomes uninhabitable, you can camp in the yard.

I shudder to think of the complete unpreparedness in light of the documented reality that isolated or large-scale disaster affects hundreds of thousands of people worldwide every year. On the other side of the scale, I would suggest that preparedness should not consume everything. You should not overburden your finances for readiness or let the risks affect your ability to enjoy your daily life.

We all try to live a balanced life. Good preparation fits this purpose well.

How to build a photovoltaic panel

What is a Photovoltaic Panel?

It is essentially a box containing a solar cell array, a set of cells connected in a certain way.

Solar cells turn sunlight into electricity.

To generate an appreciable amount of energy, many of these solar cells need to be employed; since they are very fragile, we will assemble them on a wooden panel covered with a sheet of plexiglass.

Where to Buy Solar Cells?

The first step is to purchase 36 individual 3×6 cm solar cells. By connecting the cells in series, we will build an 18 V, 3.6 A solar panel ideal for charging 12V batteries.

Once you buy cells, handle them with care; they are as thin and fragile as fragile glass, or for our Sardinian friends, cells have the same fragility as "music paper."

More giant cells (e.g., 6" x6") also exist, but it is essential to use all cells of the same size and type, as the smaller cell size may limit current.

Before proceeding to build our solar panel, I want to give you one piece of advice: to check each cell's voltage and current; this is to ensure that your panel produces maximum energy.

How to Check if a Solar Cell is Working Correctly?

Take a deep breath, and arm yourself with some patience because we are about to test whether each cell in your future panel will be able to deliver maximum power.

Only in this way can you ensure the maximum energy efficiency of your panel.

With the tester, we measure each cell's voltage and current. Simple, no?

We verify that the tester gives us values close to the values declared by the cell manufacturer. Usually, the displayed values are always a little above what we will measure.

If the tester returns us a low value in the voltage, we discard the cell immediately!

But the material that I think is best for constructing a reasonable frame is that of the standard aluminum channeling of dampers.

The conduits can be found in any hardware store.

Wireways have the following advantages: cheap, easy to cut, and immeasurably strong.

You will therefore need to get a length of at least 4 meters of conduit to be on the safe side.

As the back structure of the panel, I chose a polycarbonate honeycomb sheet that you can buy on Amazon at a great price.

This polycarbonate panel makes the structure very strong and lightweight; you can safely cut it with a typical cutter.

To protect the solar cells, the material I chose for the front of the panel is plexiglass with a UV filter, an extremely lightweight material that is easy to work with.

After cutting the four frames of our panel with an iron saw, I recommend that you file the cut edges and make sure that the frames you just created are all the size of 100cm or 50cm.

After you have soldered the aluminum wires onto all your cells, you will move on to soldering them together, as seen in the video I shot and, in the figure, next.

If you're not handy with a soldering iron, don't worry, even the most experienced people will have broken a cell; it's perfectly normal.

You'll just have to practice; after that, you'll see that you'll weld your cells professionally.

Be very gentle with the soldering iron; I used a 60-watt one.

The cells will be connected in series to give a voltage of 12Volts.

The cells will have to be connected like a serpentine, starting from the bottom left "string" you go down. The outgoing wires at the bottom will have to be associated with the first cell at the bottom of the middle string, and so going up, the first cell at the top middle will have to be connected with the first cell of the last line at the top (this in the video you can see quite well).

We solder two aluminum wires to the outgoing fins on one side of the box and the other side of the solar cells, so we will have connected all the cells in series.

Every self-respecting DIY solar panel needs to have connected in series output a Schottky diode so that during the night hours or when the Sun is missing, this diode acts as a switch by going to disconnect the panel from the battery since otherwise the battery pack would be discharged on the panel cells.

According to the specifications, the diode works best at high temperatures, so I recommend that you solder it to the wire inside the box since the temperature will certainly be higher inside our panel.

For a cleaner job, I placed the diode inside a small electrical box where I ran the panel wires out.

How to Test if the Solar Panel is Efficient? Let's test it!

Well, we've finished assembling our beloved photovoltaic panel; now we need to turn on our tester and check if we've done a workmanlike job!

To test the current, you need to insert the tester leads in series with one of the ropes coming out of the panel.

Now that we have tested the panel great, I can proceed to seal it with a bit of silicone on the entire aluminum inner structure.

Now that we have built our beautiful DIY solar panel, we cannot connect it directly to the 12-volt battery because once the battery becomes charged, the subsequent current supplied by the board would irreparably ruin our battery.

Here, then, is the need to employ a charge regulator like the one pictured on the left, which will stop charging once the battery has reached the whole charge level.

How to properly start a fire

Lighting a fire at first is not easy - especially when you are a novice. But don't worry, with the right tips and a few tricks you can learn quickly and show off all your skills on the next occasion with friends and family.

With some practice, you will come to manage your mini bonfire whenever you want.

Choose the terrain

The good idea is to build a perimeter of soil or stones around the fire. The soil should be relatively firm so that the fire does not sink in and cause a fire by attacking the roots. Ensure no flammable material is within a radius of at least three meters (including upward).

Finding good fuel

To start and maintain a fire, you need three components: bait, fuel, and feed (i.e., actual firewood).

Bait: easily flammable materials such as dry needles, dried leaves, flower fluff such as thistles, or thin wood chips are perfect for acting as "bait" for the fire. But not only that, but you can also use: mosses, lichens, bark chips, dry grass, grasses, wild cobs, dried dung of herbivores, etc.

Fuel: Spruce wood is best to get the fire started-if. That is unavailable in the area; use other thin, dry twigs.

Feed or firewood: to keep the fire going more extended, you need twigs and branches of various thicknesses. At first, feed with the thinnest twigs and gradually add thicker and thicker branches or wood. When choosing the right wood for the fire, it must be dry.

Building the brazier

Besides choosing the right fuel, proper construction of the brazier is also decisive on the success or otherwise of your fire: as a bottom layer, pile what you have collected as bait. Around this pile, you build a pyramid with thin twigs, and other wood-the thin branches go in, the thicker ones out. Leave a hole on one side through which you will light the fire in the next step.

Lighting the fire

This is where the lighter, matches, or tinder comes in. Fuel has the advantage that it always works, lighter is the lightest, and matches are easier to use.

- Protect the fire from the wind and keep the lighter as close to the bait as possible.
- As soon as the material has caught fire, blow slowly and evenly from below into the pyramid-not directly into the flames, but into the embers!
- Keep feeding the fire, ensuring that even the most significant branches are burning.
- Put more wood around the fire-don't wait too long, so it doesn't go out again.

The dimension of fire

Don't keep the fire too big, so it doesn't get out of control, but also don't keep it too small so it doesn't go out. In time you will get the right feeling.

Behaviors to observe when lighting a fire camping or in nature:

There are often designated areas for lighting fires or having barbecues. If it is an equipped campground, check with the campground managers and follow their instructions.

On the other hand, if you are free camping and the area you choose allows you to build a fire:

1. Do not light a fire too close to your tent. Tents are often made of very flammable fabrics.

2. Control the wind. Avoid creating a fire upwind to avoid having smoke and sparks in your direction or the order of flammable materials such as the tent. An important aspect is not only to prevent fire spread but also to avoid smoke poisoning.

3. Avoid flammable clothing. If you handle wood in the brazier, try to wear fireproof gloves at all times-better avoid visits to the burn center! Do not wear fleece or similar fabrics that are easily flammable.

4. Choose the place well and arrange the ground; remove leaves and similar remains that can easily catch fire. Prefer a place away from trees: there should be a space above the fire so that the smoke has the freedom to rise upward and find no obstacles.

5. Avoid using highly flammable products. DO NOT spray them directly on a burning fire; you risk exploding the container in your hands!

6. Don't leave the fire unattended, even for a short time.

7. Abandon the brazier only when the fire is entirely out. For this reason, it is helpful to keep water, even rainwater, nearby so that you can ensure all embers are no longer hot before abandoning the fire.

8. Avoid lighting fires when weather conditions may facilitate fire development, such as strong winds and intense drought.

9. Follow common sense. If you are in a predicament and need the fire to keep warm, eat, or for survival reasons, the choice between life and a fine to pay is pretty apparent;

even the forest ranger will understand the situation. If, on the other hand, the fire is just meant to be a bonus, it is a civic obligation to follow and abide by all local laws and regulations to preserve the environment.

Tips for starting a fire without a lighter

The brazier is ready; everyone is waiting for a chance to warm themselves around the fire but twist of fate: the matches and lighter are left at home! What is to be done? Do you give up? No! With a few tricks, you can still.

Starting a fire is also possible (almost) without any special tools.

Lighting a fire with a lens

The only requirement for this method: the Sun must be shining! Expose the lens or a glass bottle bottom to the light so that the beam of light is directed at the bait in your brazier. After a short time, the material should begin to burn.

Lighting a fire with a flint stone

To start a fire, you need a flint or tinder. Alternatively, you can also try striking the blade of a knife on a regular stone-the idea is to be able to create sparks. This method is especially effective if you have a piece of dry or charred wool (or cotton). This quickly absorbs the sparks, which are not dispersed unnecessarily.

Lighting a fire with a battery and some steel/aluminum wool

Although you are relatively unlikely to have a battery (preferably 9 volts) and steel wool with you, if you have forgotten your lighter, we want to introduce you to this variation:

Needed: a battery, preferably some steel wool or even a piece of aluminum.

Method: hold the steel wool or aluminum strip on both poles of the battery. If the aluminum starts to burn, keep it near the bait until the fire starts.

Lighting a fire when it is windy

Important: If the wind is mighty or if there is an official weather alert, do not light any fires! However, a light breeze is not that dangerous and is often the norm if you do not find particularly sheltered places.

Check the wind direction before lighting the fire. It is best to sit in front of the brazier so that it is shielded from the wind, and light the fire on the windward side-this gives the fire the fresh air it needs to spread. This way, there will be no uncontrolled sparks, and you will know from which direction to light the fire to prevent it from going out again.

Tip: Birch bark is a suitable fuel for moderate winds because it burns well and cannot be extinguished so quickly by the wind.

Lighting a fire when it rains

If you start a fire with wet wood, you should expect a lot of smoke.

You can start a fire even in the rain with a bit of practice. Be careful; however, wet wood can produce a lot of smoke!

The bait and fuel must be dry to make a fire in the rain. To light and start a fire, the material must be dry once started; the fire will not be affected by the rain (if the rain is not excessive, of course). If spruce trees grow in your area, you will often find dry spruce branches in the lower levels, as the trees are very dense in a crown. If you cannot find thin, dry branches, you can split a thicker piece of wood and use the dry inner splinters.

Properly extinguishing a fire

Before leaving the brazier, you should ensure that the fire is entirely out. If it is not, there is a risk that the fire will reignite unintentionally, for example, due to wind. It is best to smother the fire with sand or water if it is still burning or smoking. That also applies if you have lit the fire in a bowl because sparks can also jump out from here.

How to navigate

Orienting with the Sun

As we all know, the Sun rises in the EAST and sets in the WEST.

Knowing this, we can find North or South by observing the shadow cast by ourselves:

IN THE BOREAL HEMISPHERE (above the equator):

Around noon, the shadow cast by ourselves on the ground will always face NORTH.

IN THE AUSTRALIAN HEMISPHERE (below the equator):

Around noon, the shadow we cast on the ground will always face SOUTH.

Although it is very approximate, just remember that the Sun:

6 o'clock is in the eastern direction

9 o'clock is in the south-east

12 o'clock is in the South

3 p.m. is at South-West

6 p.m. is in the West

Remember, however, that the Sun in winter rises later and sets earlier, so it does not start precisely from the east, nor does it fully reach the West.

Orienteering with a stick and the Sun

Plant a stick in the ground, pointing it toward the Sun, so it does not cast a shadow on the floor.

After at least twenty minutes, the shadow at the base of the stick will appear; this shadow points to the east.

Wait until this shadow is at least six inches long, then draw the perpendicular to the direction of the shadow, and you will get North.

Orienteering with a clock and the Sun

The U.S. military used this method for orientation.

With the help of the Sun, one can immediately establish North with an analog clock.

IN THE BOREAL HEMISPHERE (above the equator):

Point the hour hand toward the Sun, and halfway between the hour hand and the number 12, you will find the direction of the South.

IN THE AUSTRALIAN HEMISPHERE (below the equator):

Point the number 12 (noon) dial toward the Sun, and halfway between the number 12 and the hour hand, you will find the direction of North.

Remember, however, to always do the calculation considering daylight saving time (in European Union countries, daylight saving time begins on the last Sunday in March and ends on the last Sunday in October.

During this period, for the methods described below, it is necessary to move the hour hand back one hour).

Orienteering with Compass and Map

To read the map, simply place the compass on it by matching the North and South of the compass with the North and South of the map, and you can proceed.

Orienteering with Paperless Compass

Start from a location and stop at a point of unique characteristics visible from a distance, simultaneously allowing you to see the point from which you started.

In this way, by marking the azimuth by which we see the last known point on the map, we could find our way back.

To give an example:

I leave from the spot where I set up camp and go to explore the forest.

After a short walk, always being careful not to lose sight of the field, I find a spot where there is a feature (e.g., I find myself near a large tree isolated from the rest), so I mark the azimuth by which from the point of the dry tree I can see the field.

I continue with the exploration, and as soon as I notice another point that is quite visible from a distance (e.g., a large boulder) and at the same time I see the last marked point (the isolated tree), I mark the azimuth that I read by framing it.

I will continue accordingly and stop at points characteristic in their nature and ease of view either because they are visible from a distance or because I can see the previous point clearly, marking the azimuth of the last known point from time to time.

When I wish to turn back, I will look back from the last known point and, with the help of the compass, rereading the marked degrees, retrace my steps.

Practical example:

1. Large tree isolated 45°. I see base camp
2. significant boulder 37th, large tree isolated.
3. abandoned cottage 15th and a giant boulder.

The meaning of Azimuth

It is the angular distance between North and the direction in which a point perpendicular to the horizon falls, calculated by moving clockwise.

Azimuth is not a direction but an angle.

Orienting with the stars

IN THE BOREAL HEMISPHERE (above the equator).

If it is a clear night and we can see the stars, we can look for the North Star.

It is a faintly bright star that is part of the Little Dipper; its unique feature is that it is always above the NORTH.

To find it, we try to orient ourselves this way:

We look for the constellation Cassiopeia; it is 5 pretty bright stars arranged in a zigzag pattern that, when ideally joined together, form a large W.

We now shift our gaze to our left and look a little way off for Ursa Major's constellation (also called the Big Dipper).

There are 7 very bright stars, forming the figure of a chariot with a curved rudder.

This constellation is much larger than Cassiopeia.

Now, all we have to do is ideally join the two lower stars of the giant chariot and, by extending this line five times outward, find a lone star of similar brightness to the other two stars: the North Star.

Polaris is the brightest star in the constellation Ursa Minor and is part of the seven stars of the LITTLE KARRO that lie between the two constellations of the Big Dipper and Cassiopeia.

Once the North Star is located, we have found North.

IN THE AUSTRALIAN HEMISPHERE (below the equator).

For orientation at night in the southern hemisphere, one can rely on the Southern Cross, a constellation consisting of 5 stars.

Project into the sky an imaginary line through the cross four and a half times the length, descend vertically to the horizon, and you will have found South.

Orienting with the Moon

To orient yourself with the Moon, you need to know its phases. Below is a brief hint and some mnemonic rules to remember them.

The Moon, rotating around the Earth (one full circle every 29 days), is:

New Moon (which we do not see)

First quarter (the hump is on the right)

The full Moon (all illuminated by the Sun)

Last quarter (the hump is on the left)

To remember which is the first and last quarter, you can learn the mnemonic rule that "the Moon is a liar," that is, when it looks like a C (left hump), it is Decreasing (last quarter), and when it looks like a D (right hump) it is Crescent (first quarter). Another more popular rule is "Hump to the East Waning Moon, Hump to the West Rising Moon," but it assumes that one knows the approximate direction of the East or West.

Orientation with the Moon and the clock

Use the clock with a full Moon: orient the hour hand toward the Moon; the bisector of the angle formed by the hour hand with 12 o'clock indicates South; on the opposite side will be North.

Using the clock with the Moon in the first quarter: direct the hour hand toward the Moon; the bisector formed between the direction of the Moon and 12 o'clock indicates West; rotating 90° clockwise (i.e., 3 hours past the one marking West) advises North.

Using the clock with the Moon at the last quarter: placing the clock as before the bisector will indicate the East direction, rotating 90° (i.e., 3 hours) counterclockwise will give the North advice.

Orient ourselves by observing terrain and trees

If we pay attention to the nature around us, we can still orient ourselves by following these tracks:

The north-facing part of tall trees' bark is generally covered with moss because of the increased moisture.

The growth rings are wider on the south side of the fallen tree stumps.

The foliage is thickest on the south side of the tree.

The Sun melts the snow faster toward the south-facing side.

Presence of moss on the side of the north-facing rocks.

Increased moisture in the north-facing undergrowth.

In the South, there are cleaner rubble and drier rocks.

PART 6: HYGIENE

In a survival situation, public health risks are at an all-time high.

Many substances that facilitate life quickly become deadly during hurricanes and earthquakes.

Burst pipes, falling insulation, and even dead bodies can become toxic substances impacting health.

The best choice is always to avoid public health risks. Avoid large crowds when you can, and always avoid any area that might contain toxic industrial waste or runoff.

However, one of the most significant risks will always be the human body, and you must be prepared.

Every survival bag should have at least one face mask (and today, who doesn't have at least one at home?), which will allow you to avoid many airborne pathogens.

Waste Disposal

Any good camper knows you should take only pictures and leave only memories while on the trail.

If you have evacuated your home or are in a survival situation, you must consider your waste.

Otherwise, you will not only attract predators but can cause serious health problems.

In terms of human waste, the best solution is to dig a latrine.

Make it close enough to use regularly but far enough away to avoid the smell and that runoff.

A simple latrine dug at the beginning can save you more trouble than ever imagined.

When you are finished, cover the area carefully so that others do not suffer.

Personal hygiene

Being on the move does not mean you can do without personal hygiene.

While most people think of hygiene as something you keep up with because you want to look good to others, the reality is that hygiene is essential for your health.

Therefore, it is necessary to pack basic hygiene supplies.

The minimum supplies are a bar of soap, toothpaste, and a toothbrush. Women also need to pack sanitary products (generally a one-month supply).

These supplies will keep you clean and healthy as long as you are on the move.

First, there are all those products for daily use, such as toothbrushes (even portable) and floss, shampoo and bubble bath, creams and deodorants, and you name it.

In addition to these, however, there are other products against germs and bacteria to maintain good personal hygiene even when traveling, when you do not have the opportunity to wash.

Remember, however, that these products I am about to recommend do not 100% eliminate germs and bacteria, so if we are traveling, as soon as we have a chance to wash our hands, it is good to do so.

Antibacterial gel

The antibacterial gel can be a great travel companion for staying clean; it has antiseptic power and is composed mainly of water and alcohol.

It is excellent to take on the road for any situation where you need to sanitize your hands: when we take public transportation, when we take a plane, or when we touch money.

Especially on an airplane, it is most beneficial to avoid constantly going **to the bathroom** to wash your hands with soap and water. Here's what to bring when traveling to take care of personal hygiene.

Sanitizing wipes

Most people use this product. Sanitizing wipes are helpful and ready to use, and we can use them to sanitize hands and any surface, such as the remote control we find in our hotel rooms, seats, and armrests of trains and airplanes.

Germicidal lamp

This tool is not yet well known, but it is perfect for its ability to eliminate germs. That could also be an excellent ally to take with us on trips because it is:

- small
- handy
- light

But what is this product? The germicidal lamp produces ultraviolet light that can kill various viruses, germs, and bacteria. A unique and very effective tool that not everyone has and is great for those who love hygiene and cleanliness.

We can opt for defatting or regenerating creams but also massage creams and oils, perhaps for a moment of complete detachment from the outside world. Another product that should never be missing from our suitcase is dental floss, which is valuable and convenient to carry everywhere.

Let us also not forget that mosquitoes have arrived at this time, and if we are going to a reasonably humid place, it is good to bring the appropriate repellent spray against these little critters that everyone hates. In addition to the things to pack we should also be careful to avoid some bad attitudes.

One tip is to avoid sharing towels or toothbrushes, even among couples or close relatives. As you can imagine, there can be an easy exchange of germs.

Other useful things:

Towel: must not be missing to avoid skin contact with loungers or deck chairs.

Sunscreen: essential for protecting our skin against the sun's rays.

Spare swimsuit: It is not recommended to keep it wet due to germ proliferation.

False myths about personal hygiene

Not all hygiene methods act in the way we think; in fact, there are some false myths about some classic habits. As the first false myth, let's talk about soap.

Then let's talk about hand sanitizers, which have become our daily routine and are often substituted for hand washing. What exactly does it do? Does it kill germs? I would have to say no. It simply tries to promote their elimination from the surface of the skin. The soap then encompassed the germs and rinsed away by the water.

If they are accompanied by washing with soap, they can be an excellent ally against germs, but if used as the only choice, they are not entirely practical.

Hygiene is a science within medicine that studies the reactions and interactions between human beings and their environment, focusing specifically on the norms and measures to promote collective health. We delve into the usefulness of this discipline and why it is essential to follow its guidelines.

Hygiene for disease prevention

The main reason for using medical devices and cosmetic products for hygiene is that good cleanliness of the body and what we come into contact with helps prevent the infection of diseases. Of course, this has been added-especially in more industrialized countries-a purely cosmetic function: total intimate depilation, for example, is not recommended by hygiene experts, yet it is a fad that many people demand.

Commonly used products for personal hygiene

What can we do individually to improve our hygiene and that of the environment in which we live? The pharmaceutical and cosmetics industry is thriving more than ever, offering us endless personal care and household cleaning products. Drawing not only on synthetic active ingredients, typical of medicines, but also on the properties of natural products, which are less aggressive but just as effective. Shampoo, bubble bath, soap, toothpaste, disinfectant, sanitizing, and anti-mold sprays are all readily available products that help us maintain a high level of hygiene.

Hygiene rules are not to be underestimated.

More than products, it is often healthy habits that make the difference. There are certain behaviors, in fact, that, if done regularly, allow us to prevent disease and live in a healthier body and environment. Among them:

- Frequent hand washing is the easiest way to avoid contamination
- Sneezing or coughing with the hand in front is critical to prevent germs from spreading
- Airing out the environment where you live or work is the best prevention weapon against infection.

Living in a healthy environment

Hygiene is not just about taking care of oneself: it is only natural that the environment around us should also be healthy. Poor waste disposal, food storage, and construction materials are harmful to health. The condition of pets or animals for human consumption and, of course, environmental pollution are, all factors that need to be kept under strict control to ensure that what we eat and the places where we are not harmful to our health. All of this, however, is our responsibility, and it is, therefore, necessary to follow the most up-to-date hygienic standards to live at our best. Stay informed about medical, building, and environmental innovations that promote hygiene and learn about good habits to follow for healthy living.

Shelter sanitation and preventive medicine

If natural disasters forced people to be crammed into basements and appropriate shelters for days or weeks, they would have to protect themselves from spreading infectious diseases by taking habitual and unusual preventive measures. Disease prevention would become much more important if modern medical facilities were temporarily unavailable.

The infection prevention in the following chapter measures are simple, practical, and require self-discipline.

PART 7: FIRST AID AND NATURAL MEDICINE

First aid kit

A first aid kit is necessary for all emergencies; family members are prone to injury and illness during these disasters. Your kit should include all the required medicines and equipment. It should have everything needed for wound care and a pamphlet on first aid techniques.

Make sure your first aid kit includes:

- Bandages, cotton swabs, elastic bands, gauze, and medical tapes. These items will help if abrasions or sprains occur. A box of sterilized strips can help close more significant cuts.

- Denatured alcohol, peroxide, and witch hazel. These can be used to clean wounds.

- Aspirin. Aspirin reduces fever and relieves pain.

- Antidiarrheal drugs. Many biological and pandemic episodes will have diarrhea associated with the effects of the virus. Having these types of over-the-counter medications will be very helpful.

- Multivitamins. You should pack more vitamins so all affected people can maintain their strength. You may be unable to eat healthy during this time, and the vitamins will make sure you stay well nourished.

- Cough and cold medicines. A multipurpose medicine will come in handy if symptoms arise.

- Soap. Make sure you have soap bars in your medical supplies. It will be essential to wash your hands in case of bioterrorism or pandemic.

- Prescription drugs. If you have time to prepare for the event, call your doctor and request an extra month of prescription medication.

First aid and medicines: keep healthy

First aid books pose an interesting problem.

On the one hand, they are undoubtedly helpful: knowing how to identify or treat an injury is a great advantage, especially if not everyone in your group is trained in first aid.

Unfortunately, these books are often bulky and take up space in your backpack that might be better served by carrying other equipment.

The best solution is to find a small pocket first aid booklet. Look for something geared toward wilderness survival, particularly camping treatments for wounds.

Basic information on how to dress a wound, deal with an infection, or perform basic field procedures will be best.

Take the time to memorize as much as possible and ensure everyone in the group with you does the same.

You don't need anything with advanced medical information: the unfortunate truth is that the field is simply not the right place to learn how to perform surgery on yourself.

Medical kits and containers

When traveling, you need to find a storage solution for your medications.

An excellent first aid kit should be the package, but finding something sturdier might be ideal.

A good solution for storing a first aid kit is a drumstick bag: available for about twenty dollars at most music stores, these canvas bags take up little space but have enough room to hold an entire first aid kit inside.

Most of the rules that apply to food containers will apply to drugs. Make sure everything you use is airtight and leak-proof.

You should also make sure that any storage solution is labeled so that you and your group can understand what is in it but others cannot.

Medicines can be precious, so there is no need to advertise your wealth.

Medicines and drugs

You must take proper precautions and pack medications to help you during evacuation or survival.

Start by researching common ailments that people experience when they travel, and also make sure you know the various ailments that affect people in your area.

Make sure, for example, that you know which plants are poisonous and which contagious infections may occur along your path (e.g., you should recognize the types of fungi and the plants from which to make medicines).

Pack one of the medications that should help you with these problems, and consider investing in any kind of preventive product that will help strengthen your immune system.

Finally, make sure you know your medical allergies. Having penicillin on hand is a good idea, but not if you are allergic.

If you are allergic to essential medications, pack an alternative (I recommend allergen testing as soon as possible).

Even more important, be sure to pack something that will let others know about your allergies.

Customization

You are the best judge of what you need to survive. When it comes to medicine, no one can give you a perfect bag; you have to figure out what you need for yourself.

The best way to figure out what you need is to do a small test yourself. A pencil and a pad of paper are the only tools you will need.

Take a week to determine the medications you use. Look at all prescriptions and determine how often they need to be refilled.

If you use any over-the-counter medication, you should try to figure out what dosage you need over the course of a week.

If you use any kind of conditioner or other products, consider them in your packing plans. Everything you need for your health should go with you.

There is nothing wrong with packing extra medication, but you must figure out what you can live without. If you can wean yourself off of anything, try to do it over time.

You should also try to find alternatives for any medication that is hard to find or has a short expiration date you never know when or if you will be able to find it again, especially if you should find yourself in a long-term survival situation.

Prepping is not an easy path, but it is worth all the effort it takes to get there. It is a significant effort and just as essential as any other part of a well-structured preparedness plan. One component, in particular, may be pretty tricky for some people to consider. It seems medicine is probably the most critical area in the realm of preparedness where people of our time might avoid the notion of self-sufficiency.

For some, it may be a degree of apprehension. Modern medicine, after all, is one of our most extraordinary resources. Members of the medical community represent the best and brightest in society. They have spent years of specialized education and training to earn their credentials.

Their work requires a steady hand, intelligence, care, and trust. There is often little room for error.

Meanwhile, those who work in emergency response make a living in high-stress environments with higher stakes. They are ready to move the minute a call comes in. It is incredible to think about the balance and focus that all of our medical professionals maintain out of habit when people are suffering or lives are at stake.

Injuries and illnesses are complex for many to think about. Taking responsibility for a person's well-being may involve intimidation. It requires calm and courage. It is easy to see how most people out there might cringe at making it themselves.

Preppers, however, understand how quickly life could change for the worse. The best or most favorable option is not always available. Everything we usually rely on, including medical care, could disappear instantly. It has already happened and will inevitably happen again.

You may run into a situation where you are forced to provide your care. You might get lost, put yourself in danger, and have no chance for help beyond the supplies carried in your backpack. A call to emergency services could not offer relief if you were in a desolate location out of reach of cell phone reception. You would be on your own if you were to trip and significantly injure your leg on a jagged rock. You should take your first aid kit. Knowing how to properly use the goods packed inside would be critical.

The community may find itself reeling after an act of nature. The situation would provide less panic, pain, and difficulty if we or a loved one knew how to apply a splint that would suffice in the meantime.

Regarding self-sufficiency, all people should have at least a minimal ability to offer the best in terms of assistance should time and necessity eventually call for it.

The rule of three is not about what makes you comfortable. It is about survival. People could easily find themselves having to survive without the help and knowledge of doctors.

Any fraction of knowledge is better than none. Even basic first aid skills could give you a natural ability to restore calm in an otherwise hectic situation. At the very least, you could provide the injured person a better ability to wait for more substantial intervention. Understanding illnesses and their causes would allow you to steer your family away from some pretty significant dangers. Disasters often bring risk at every turn.

Preppers should not go beyond the basics. You would not need to take the path toward a degree in nursing or medicine. Having a solid base of preparation would not require you to obtain an emergency medical technician license. A prepper would not attempt self-surgery. It is not about knowing everything. It is simply a matter of knowing enough.

Health is always a significant concern after a disaster. Preparedness, in general, is an exercise in taking charge of our well-being.

The aftermath of some pretty recent disasters illustrates the atypical risks that those struggling might encounter after calm re-emerges. More significant trauma risks would exist because of all the scattered rubble and debris. Diseases are known to settle in communities in the weeks and months following a disaster.

Any emergency means a heavier workload for anyone making a career of serving the public. Often, a disaster means our professionals have more work and far less ability to handle it. Hospitals may play a more important role than many buildings in our communities, but they are as susceptible to damage as any other.

Preparation means reaching reasonable solutions at the individual level before the problems documented elsewhere hit home. It is a matter of attitude. Post-disaster safety and the potential need to treat injuries require effort and the right mindset.

All people, preppers or not, should take the time to become certified in CPR. CPR may provide the only opportunity to save another's life if he or she is pulseless and not breathing. It could be a heart attack. It could be any number of other causes. The courses last only a few hours and offer the potential to save a person whose very life depends on a few critical minutes.

This skill is as important for every day as it is for disaster. You should never assume someone else would have the skills to take on that critical life-saving task in a time of need. It comes back to self-reliance. It is a small amount of time that is spent incredibly well.

Everyone should take basic and advanced first aid courses. They would allow you to handle potential trauma in the wake of disaster. First aid training, such as CPR, also provides an excellent everyday skill set. Accidents happen. Medical conditions always put people in critical danger. Those trained in first aid have the vital ability to initiate care in those all-important minutes before an ambulance arrives.

Considering all the good that could come from a small amount of training is essential. Treating even a minor injury could provide the injured person with calm and comfort until they can see a professional. That good would extend further in having the ability to treat an injury during chaotic times when risks abound, and there is no guarantee that any professional will arrive quickly. A trainer could offer the injured person his or her best chance.

Enrollees learn how to manage a bleed. Lessons range from cleaning and dressing a simple cut to properly using a tourniquet that would stop significant bleeding after a potentially critical injury. The full range of these skills could become very important. It is easy to imagine encountering wounds of varying severity among wrecks immediately after a disaster or as cleanup progresses.

Courses would teach you how to handle minor bone breaks. Studies would address the treatment of burns and sprains. You would learn how to care for those suffering from seizures or heat- or cold-related emergencies.

This valuable information fits well with the broader scope of emergency planning.

Supplies become essential as they relate to potential injuries. It is vital to have a sufficiently stocked first aid kit on hand. First aid kits are a critical piece of the trainer's kit.

Each kit would include the basics, including a good supply of bandages, gauze, and painkillers. Many would decide to pack a tourniquet and do so with the firm hope that they would never encounter wounds so severe that they would require its use. As far as disaster preparedness is concerned, a good kit would include a decent supply of triple antibiotic cream for use even on more minor cuts.

Proper wound cleaning and dressing are essential every day. It is more so during a survival situation or after a disaster. A prepper would recognize the rapid and severe difficulties that infection could pose and the complications it would bring to the overall efforts required following a disaster. You cannot take chances.

The knowledge offered through first aid courses and the skills provided by kits offers a prepper greater personal benefit when he or she recognizes that the primary goal of prepping is simply to stay alive. Injury or illness could severely limit your chances of surviving a survival situation. The rest of your preparations could not make a difference.

Preparation in its entirety is a practice of maintaining vigilance, and there is no area in which it is more important than health. Our health is the most important thing we have.

Doctors are intelligent people. Their advice is worth following. It is especially true for all those frequently repeated messages that too often fall on deaf ears. Put down the cigarettes. Avoid fast food. Step away from the TV screen and get moving.

Those already struggling with certain health conditions would like to keep their own when working through recovery. You should recognize your limitations and be careful not to take unnecessary risks whenever possible.

The medical side of preparedness is undoubtedly not one of the most accessible pieces of the prepper lifestyle. Maintaining health is a part of prepping that comes into play through daily decisions.

It is frightening to confront the possibility of injury or health problems. It is even more challenging to consider encountering these difficulties without having a hand within our qualified medical community. The best remedy for fear is always action.

Get to work now, and you will be able to provide for yourself later. It all starts with attitude. If a painful, though not life-threatening, injury were to occur, you would be able to rely on the skills, knowledge, and confidence that were opened up through learning long before the emergency occurred.

It is doable. People throughout history have done everything before. Preparation is a practice that recognizes how much we can accomplish with the right effort.

You might think back to those encouraging words we heard growing up, "You can do anything if you put your mind to it."

Preparation is taking charge. It is coming to recognize that we can take care of ourselves. It recognizes that nothing good can come from simply ignoring the facts. Bad things happen frequently. They could happen to us. What can we do, then?

You can gain a lot of strength when you recognize how much you can do on your own. We can make a good life for ourselves and our families no matter what Mother Nature puts in our paths. It's just a matter of thinking and following through to ensure our basic needs are covered for tomorrow, just as today.

Preparation makes a lot of sense for those who have their families' best interests in mind. It is an intelligent path to take.

It is the very definition of freedom. It is about going our way and meeting our own needs as we see fit. It is about getting the job done without waiting for someone else.

You could choose the easy path and be content to rely on others. You could make some extra effort and desire the freedom to do it your way.

Natural medicines

Echinacea for the immune system

ECHINACEA

With the first colds, especially during the change of season, echinacea is a valuable aid in strengthening the immune system. In particular, this plant belonging to the Compositae family contains polysaccharides with immune-stimulating action. Therefore, it is used in herbal medicine to strengthen the natural defenses and the immune system, thereby supporting the body against viruses and bacteria. For internal use, you should take echinacea in cycles of up to 8 weeks with a one-month break between cycles during seasonal changes.

Fennel seeds against abdominal bloating

Fiber, vitamins, and essential oils are why fennel seeds are so important. We should not call them that because they are not seeds but flowers. Their carminative action can reduce pain related to abdominal bloating and counteract aerophagia. In herbal tea, fennel seeds stimulate digestion and promote intestinal motility.

Hawthorn, plant of the heart

Hawthorn grows wild in our regions, and from its leaves and flowers, we can derive the properties that make this fragrant shrub an effective natural anxiolytic and soother. Flavonoids, antioxidants present in reasonable quantities, allow cardioprotective action by inducing dilation of the arteries leading to the heart and thus lowering blood pressure. Taken in herbal tea, it could contribute to the proper functioning of the cardiovascular system in cases of tachycardia, extrasystoles, and arrhythmias.

St. John's Wort against sunburn

ST JOHN'S WORT

St. John's Wort is also a wild plant readily available. St. John's wort is used for its flowering stems, which contain antioxidants such as hypericin, which could improve mood, as a natural sedative, and as a natural anti-depressant. This agent is suitable for internal and external use for various purposes. The oil, ole olive, and creams are mainly used as an anti-inflammatory to medicate minor skin wounds and against sunburn. It's best to consult your doctor, pharmacist, or herbalist regarding intake for internal use, as St. John's wort can create numerous interactions with medications and other supplements. External use isn't recommended before sun exposure due to photosensitizing compounds.

Be careful: This plant can interact with contraceptives, so use with care.

Chamomile for natural suffumigation

Queen of bedtime herbal teas, chamomile contains coumarins, flavonoids, and essential oil, which have different modes of use in phytotherapy. It acts as a natural muscle relaxant, reducing pain caused by abdominal cramps, dysmenorrhea, and muscle spasms. Its anti-inflammatory effect is also effective for inflammation of the skin and mucous membranes, bacterial infections, and respiratory tract irritation. Chamomile is used in this regard to naturally choke the respiratory tract. Chamomile compresses constitute home first aid in cases of eczema and conjunctivitis.

CHAMOMILE

Sage for menstrual pain

Sage

We owe much to Salvia Officinalis: this fragrant evergreen is rich in essential oil, terpenes, tannins, and flavonoids. In phytotherapy, it is a woman's faithful ally. In cases of dysmenorrhea and amenorrhea, it helps regulate the menstrual cycle and intervenes to soothe pain when taken as a mother tincture. Also, during the aliphatic phase of the arrival of menopause, this medicinal plant thanks to its estrogenic action, reduces the occurrence of excessive sweating and "hot flashes" thanks to its rebalancing intervention at the hormonal level.

Licorice for the stomach

Licorice is a perennial plant that did not reach Europe until after the 15th century. This root is attributed to anti-inflammatory, diuretic, digestive, expectorant, and protective action on the gastric mucosa.

It acts on the respiratory tract by disinflaming the throat in cases of coughs and when there is the presence of phlegm. It is a natural disinflammatory, and its expectorant power allows it to increase the production of prostaglandins with a protective effect on the stomach. In contrast to hawthorn, however, it is indicated for improving blood pressure.

Ginkgo biloba for concentration

Ginkgo biloba is a plant in the Ginkgoaceae family. It contains terpenes, phenols, and flavonoids that counteract forming free radicals, precursors of cellular aging. The ability to promote the proper distribution of oxygen and glucose to the brain attributed to this plant improves mental activity by aiding concentration and short-term memory, which is why ginkgo Biloba is well suited for study and intellectual work. And not only that, the active substances effectively combat the onset and development of neurodegenerative diseases such as Alzheimer's.

Devil's claw against muscle and joint pain

The analgesic and anti-inflammatory efficacy of harpagosides contained in devil's claw root are believed to be responsible for the plant's analgesic and antipyretic effects. Joint pains such as back pain, cervical arthritis, headache, and muscle and joint pain of an inflammatory nature such as arthritis or tendinitis can be relieved by external application of devil's claw ointment.

Ginseng, against stress

When stress and physical and mental fatigue arise, a full tank of ginseng is the solution you need. A natural stress reliever thanks to adaptogenic properties that strengthen the immune, endocrine, and nervous systems. The athlete will appreciate its stimulating property resulting in improved reflexes and physical endurance made possible by ginsenosides, saponins extracted from the roots with adaptogenic and exciting action.

Ginseng

PART 8: KNOT TYING GUIDE

Stopping knots

Stopping knots are tied at the ends of ropes to prevent them from slipping out of holes or blocks. The most basic application of arrest knots is the knot used to hold the thread in the eye of the needle.

In seamanship, arrest knots are used in current rigging (sheets, halyards, etc.) and for decorative purposes on prominent lines. Some of them, such as the monkey fist, can be used as weighting knots for lines or throwing lines. The most critical stopping knots are the simple knot, the Savoy knot, the Capuchin knot, the Franciscan knot, and the monkey fist.

Origins

The simple knot is a stopping node. It is the most common example of a node in a general sense.

The simple knot has remote origins, probably prehistoric; think of the Peruvian quipu, which testifies to the existence of a type of writing performed using superficial knots along a rope.

In ancient times, the knot was considered a demonic tool and a symbol endowed with magical powers. In folklore, the knot has been attributed to the authority to bind the spirit to the earth.

Strengths and weaknesses

The simple knot, also called a single knot, when tied at the end of the rope, is a secure knot, but it has the defect of tightening too much, damaging the fibers of the line. For this reason, it is difficult to untie, mainly when the rope is wet. It is a knot rarely used in boating.

Applications

The simple knot combines the arresting function with keeping a body tied when the two ends of the rope are under tension; otherwise, the knot would untie very easily. Its presence on rescue ropes at regular intervals makes climbing easier. Finally, it is the essential element for creating more complex knots.

Junction knots

Since immemorial, man has used junction knots in the most elementary occurrences: for building huts, joining lianas, animal traps, primitive weapons, for weaving. Joint knots are asked for ease of being untied after use and to be able to join the ends of two ropes without damaging their texture, replacing the splice. Such knots, therefore, can use the same wires or ropes several times.

For splicing knots to provide a certain degree of safety, it is necessary for the ropes used to have the same diameter and the same properties. An exception to this rule is the flag knot, which, although it joins two ropes of different diameters and nature, is equally safe.

The most crucial splicing knots are:

- The flat knot.
- The sheet or flag knot.
- The cow knot.
- The English knot.
- The double English knot.
- The two gasses.

For some joining knots, there is the possibility of hooking, which consists of a doublet forming an eye added to the knot itself. The most critical granted knots are: the flat granted knot, called the terzaruol or mutation knot, and the flag awarded knot.

There are other joining knots, with different characteristics from those used in the maritime art, which, when tightened, can no longer untie. The best known are the weaver's knot and the net knot.

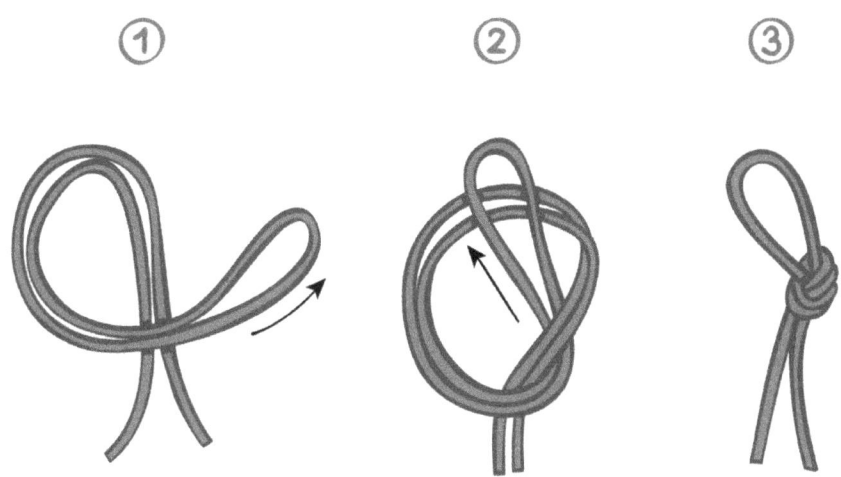

Sheet knot or flag

Such a knot owes its name to its intended use.

It is called a sheet knot because it connects the sheets, the rope used to orient the sail, with special eyelets located at the ends of square sails. It is also called a flag knot because, with two flag knots, the lower and upper lots of the flags are precisely connected.

Strengths and weaknesses

The merits of the sheet knot or flag knot are: joining two ropes of different diameters and nature, quick execution, not slipping, not tightening, and offering greater strength when subjected to solid tension.

The greatest merit of this knot is undoubtedly that it can join two ropes of different diameters; however, this does not detract from the fact that it cannot be used profitably in joining lines of equal diameter.

Applications

This knot is used in boating on current rigging, to connect elbows, lines, shrouds, and stays; in mountaineering to connect two ropes even of different diameters; in camping to put tension on guy lines, to hang hammocks, etc.

Eye knots

Eye knots, or gasse, are loops that are closed and knotted almost generally, at the end of a rope. Unlike winding knots, which are made directly on the object, these knots are almost always made in hand and then passed around a bollard, hook, or pole. Moreover, eye knots do not spill or fail when slipped off the object, and, since their shape is not determined by the object around which they are wrapped, they can be used repeatedly.

The main eye knots are the lover's bowline, double and triple lover's bowline, double-rope lover's bowline; Spanish bowline; hooked lover's bowline; and fisherman's loop.

Gassa D'Amante

The gassa d'amante is known as the queen of knots because it is the most critical knot in maritime art; you are not a good sailor if you do not know how to make gassa d'amante quickly and, if necessary, in the dark.

The knot is executed differently depending on whether it faces the person executing it or in the opposite direction.

Strengths and weaknesses

The main merit of this knot is that it is not a slipknot and does not tighten too much; also, while it is a very secure knot, the lover's bowline can be untied easily, even when the line is wet. Such a knot can be tied with all types of cord.

Applications

In boating it's used for man overboard recovery, on jib sheets, mooring to the bollard, forming a hoist, downhaul, hoisting sails, landing large mooring lines, etc.

In mountaineering, the gassa d'amanta is known as Bulin's knot and is used for simple lifetime tie-downs. From this knot we derive other ways of rope tying that are essential on challenging climbs, e.g., Bulin's double-brace knot, which, in the event of a fall, distributes the strain over the climber's entire torso, preventing severe internal injury.

Scorsoi knots

These knots are also called nooses or ties. Their characteristic is that they tighten around the objects on which they are made: the more pressure exerted on the rope, the stronger the slipknot tightens the object around which it is wrapped.

Strengths and weaknesses

The fact that the grip of slipknots is directly proportional to rope tension is more of a flaw than merit. This characteristic limit their use in cases where one is well assured that the rope tension is constant; conversely, the loosening of the rope tension makes scores of knots extremely unsafe. In conclusion, apart from well-defined uses, it is advisable to avoid using slipknots. The safer eye knots from which they are ultimately derived should be preferred.

Origins

Slipknots rank among the oldest knots known to man: since prehistoric times, man has used them as traps to catch animals. The main scorsoi knots are: the simple slipknot, the gassa d'amante scorsoia. As a curiosity, we also show the hangman's knot.

Knots

For no reason in the world should a rope be cut? A cut rope has lost much value, and no splicing knot can restore it to its primitive qualities of safety and usability.

When the length of the rope is abundant for a particular use, one can resort to shortening knots, which, as the name implies, are used to shorten ropes without resorting to cutting them.

A particular use of shortening knot is to exclude using the worn or damaged parts that the rope should have. Those parts are included in the shortening knot, remain inoperative, and consequently excluded from any effort.

Strengths and weaknesses

The merits of shortening knots derive from the uses most described above. In contrast, they have some shortcomings, which will be examined by illustrating individual knots. The main shortening knots are the Daisy knot, the simple doublet knot with a bowline.

Winding knots

Winding knots are generally performed directly on an object, either to secure something on it or to tighten a rope around it. It is a good rule while executing the vaults to follow the direction of twisting the rope. Winding knots are divided into two groups: the first group is those knots performed by passing the rope around the object two or more times and inserting current and sleeper under the vaults.

The second group belongs to those knots performed by passing the rope around the object two or more times and knotting the current around the sleeper with half-necks. They belong to the first group: the single, double and triple speech (on a rod or ring), the ganciato speech, the wolf's mouth, the gallaccio knot, and the ganciato gallaccio knot. Belonging to the second group: half-necks, ganciato half-neck, anchor knot, double and triple, draft knot.

Utility applications and bindings

The art of knot tying has always been important to all peoples, and even in ancient times, man knew the usefulness of this art.

Even today, some tribes build their huts and canoes and prepare traps and tools by knotting ropes with reed frames.

In addition to utility ligatures, there are decorative ligatures, constituting a true art of knot tying.

This art, which among the folk arts is among the oldest, was spread by sailors, who are rightly believed to be the connoisseurs of knots. In tying a knot, different types of knots are tied: winding, splicing, stopping, etc., to tie a knot. However, it is not enough to tie a series of knots. It is necessary to know the ropes' nature and how to handle them.

This art, which among the folk arts is among the oldest, was spread by sailors, who are rightly believed to be the connoisseurs of knots. In tying a knot, different types of knots are tied: winding, splicing, stopping, etc., to tie a knot. However, it is not enough to tie a series of knots. It is necessary to know the ropes' nature and how to handle them.

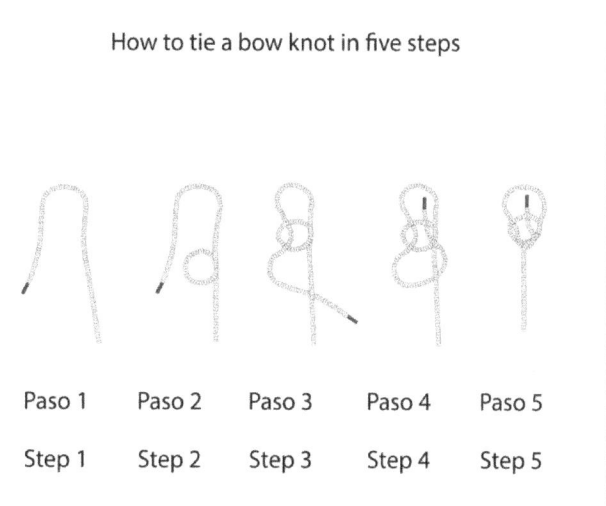

How to tie a bow knot in five steps

| Paso 1 | Paso 2 | Paso 3 | Paso 4 | Paso 5 |
| Step 1 | Step 2 | Step 3 | Step 4 | Step 5 |

PART 9: THE IMPORTANCE OF THE COMMUNITY

Many sociological and psychological studies have investigated the sense of community and also established some ways or indicators to be able to detect it while in a situation of emergency.

One of its definitions is as follows: "A feeling that members have of belonging, of bonding with each other and with the group, of shared confidence that their own and others' needs will be met through shared effort" - McMillan and Chavis.

As mentioned at the beginning of this article, a sense of community is essential in strengthening, uniting, and coping with events that can affect the whole community and even the individual. It is a valuable practical and psychological source of social and individual well-being.

It is not a quick and easy building process; sometimes, even maintaining it requires much effort from institutions and individuals.

Another aspect to consider is the subjectivity of the perception of this feeling; it may be that there is a strong and general sense of community among citizens, but one individual does not feel it so strongly and does not value the community as a resource.

When we talk about community, we do not mean only the village, territorial, or only the one where there are many people. Even a numerically smaller community such as the school, classroom, workplace, or family community can take on the same functions.

One way to break down and analyze the sense of community is to break it down into four different but interconnected factors:

Belonging: that feeling of being part of something is traced in customs, territorial, or historical-cultural boundaries such as wards. The person feels that he or she is part of a group and perceives acceptance from other members.

Increasing membership requires a personal commitment to the group and community, such as volunteering or helping prepare some city events. Membership generates a sense of emotional security of high importance to the individual.

Influence corresponds to that feeling of actually being able to impact the community and group. Also, perceiving some control is essential to be attracted to that group.

A sense of control toward the group must be balanced with the group's control, understood as conformity, over the individual. A kind of dance between group and individual. In any case, there can be no active participation if there is no perception in the individual that he or she can contribute something, modify or affect in some way toward his or her community or territory; thanks also to those intellectual, cultural, religious and professional diversities that the individual possesses.

Integration and satisfaction of needs, people feel part of a community toward which they feel secure in the satisfaction of their practical and psychological needs; satisfaction of needs in interdependence and dialogue among community members.

Ultimately, there is a need to develop and maintain a shared emotional connection. This is created when the previous conditions exist and, in turn, reinforce them in a virtuous cycle. This emotional bond binds the members of a group varies with the number and quality of relationships among the various individuals.

As said during the conference and thinking about the Municipality of St. Casciano, events such as the medieval carnival, the carnival of the little ones, the wards, the associations, and even the individual events in the hamlets are all activities that enhance individuals a sense of community. In our huge protective factors even during periods of economic and social disruption such as the current one.

Volunteer or economic activities aimed at and embedded in the community are also functional and necessary if they incorporate the factors of belonging, influence, integration, and a shared emotional connection.

The moment a sense of community is created, sustained, and fostered even toward new inhabitants, a virtuous circle is set in motion that can multiply the social capital of any community, a village, hamlet, the workplace, through its factors in the school and the family.

Fundamental point and as has been explained above, for a sense of community to be created requires commitment from the individual and the community, little or nothing is made if only one-party acts toward the other.

PART 10: THE PREPPER'S COOKBOOK

The time has finally come to use up all that food you've been putting in your pantry! Thanks to this cookbook, you can make new and super yummy recipes with simple ingredients that you most likely already own.

When you find yourself in a momentary emergency or survival situation, your creativity is the only thing you need to make great dishes.

You don't need superfine, hard-to-find ingredients; simple cooking is always the best and most appreciated by everyone.
So, the only ingredients you will need are canned food (which you will surely have set aside) and some spices and herbs to flavor your dishes.

I want to point out that some recipes also contain fresh ingredients that, if you have the chance, you can use; otherwise, you might as well do less of them or replace them with some frozen, dried, or powdered ingredients.

The main goal here is still to get a reasonable caloric intake to keep your health and physique fit, so below, you will find mainly recipes with high carbohydrate and protein content, which are essential to staying fit and having much energy.

Below you will find some of the best recipes you can cook with the canned and shelf-stable food in your pantry. The recipes that follow have been chosen for these two main reasons:

- They are great recipes to fill your stomach.
- They do not require too many pots and utensils for preparation.

I am sure you will appreciate this cookbook in case you are in an emergency and forced to cook only with the ingredients you have at home; here comes to your rescue this cookbook!

Don't forget one essential thing: food also significantly impacts your mood, which consequently affects how you feel, so the taste is also definitely not to be overlooked when cooking.

Another advantage of cooking only with simple, shelf-stable ingredients is that they are almost undoubtedly healthy foods (for example, legumes, flours, vegetables, rice, pasta, etc.) without those chemicals that do nothing but harm your body. You will then get back to detoxing from the junk food you were used to.

All preppers need to have canned food in their food pantry. Canned food not only lasts for several years but is also the only food that can withstand water floods, earthquakes, and other natural disasters. If the boxes remain unopened, the food inside will remain safe.

In addition, there are plenty of canned food items: vegetables, legumes, meat, fish, and fruit. You can have virtually any food you need with a long shelf life.
So, try to make an ample supply of canned food, and don't forget the can opener!

Without wasting any more time, I'll leave you with the best recipes you can prepare and enjoy.

MEAT PRESERVATION - SALTING

How to preserve meat in the absence of a refrigerator thanks to salting.

Certainly, preserving by salting can be helpful when you do not have the option of using a refrigerator or freezer to store meat. In such a situation, you can go back in time and preserve food as when the preservation methods today did not exist.

Salting allows you to preserve food by removing the water inside, thus blocking the vital functions of microorganisms.

A disadvantage of this preservation method is that it results in a loss of food nutrients.

Ingredients:

5 pounds of beef

1 cup of salt

1 cup molasses

1/2 tablespoon cloves

1/2 tablespoon of black pepper

1 tablespoon saltpeter

Procedure:

Combine all the ingredients in a bowl and mix. Then you need to spread the mixture all over the meat, covering it well. The next step is to let the meat rest for about 10 days, remembering that it should be turned daily.

CURED BACON ROLLED UP

You should know that seasoned bacon was a popular food in the past when travelers had to travel. The reason is simple, it was easy to prepare and could be stored for a sufficiently long time.

The best time to prepare seasoned bacon, and in general all preparations that do not involve the use of the refrigerator, is always best during the winter because the cold weather helps to season.

Ingredients:

1 kg fresh bacon

18g-20g salt

1-2g of black pepper

1 clove (optional)

Grated nutmeg (optional)

1g crumbled cinnamon (optional)

1 clove of garlic (optional)

As you can see, some of the ingredients are optional because you may not necessarily possess these ingredients, so if you don't have them, you can still proceed with preparing the bacon.

Procedure:

Trim the bacon by removing excess fat.

The next step is to prepare the "seasoning," mixing all the dry ingredients used to flavor and preserve the bacon. Spread the seasoning all over the meat, trying to cover them well. Next, you need to roll the bacon well with the fat towards the outside, leaving no air inside (this aspect is crucial). Once rolled, you need to close the bacon with a food string or elastics. The meat should turn out as tight as possible.

It is now ready to season. Hang the bacon to drain at room temperature for 3 days. Then turn it upside down and allow another 3 days to pass.

The last step is to put the bacon in the season for at least 90 days in a cool place.

After this time has passed, it will be possible to consume raw or cooked bacon to flavor other foods.

HOW TO PREPARE DRIED MEAT AT HOME

In this recipe, we will see how to prepare homemade jerky. Thanks to this preservation method, you can increase the shelf life and consume it whenever you want.

Ingredients:

Beef (preferably shoulder or breast)

Salt

Spices to taste

Procedure:

Clean the meat of fat, removing as much of it as possible but without digging in and ruining the meat. The next step is to cut the meat into slices (note: cut the meat in the opposite direction to the fibers; otherwise, it will be chewy and difficult to chew) and then later into thin strips.

If necessary, you can help yourself by freezing the meat slices first and then cutting them from frozen; it will be easier to cut them.

Now let's move on to the seasoning; lightly salt the meat and season it with the spices of your choice. Then next, you need to spread the meat on an open baking sheet that will allow the juices to drip out. Turn the oven to the lowest permitted temperature (between 140°F - 170°F) and let the meat cook for about 5-6 hours.

To check if the cooking is completed, check if the meat still has liquids or juices inside; it should not drip or release moisture on your hands by opening or folding it. Once the meat is ready, turn off the oven, and let the heat and moisture escape. Let the jerky rest overnight before it can be stored.

MEAT STEW

This is a straightforward recipe that is very versatile and that your stomach will surely enjoy as well. Meat stew is a dish that provides much protein. You can also accompany it with rice or grains to your liking. You can add bacon to give this dish an extra touch if you like.

Preparation time: 5 min

Cooking time: 30 min

Ingredients:

Canned or dried vegetables

Canned or dried meat

Spices

Water or broth

Flour or cornstarch (for thickening)

Procedure:

Combine all ingredients in the pot and cook over low heat until well hydrated and tender. If necessary, thicken the stew with flour or cornstarch.

For quantities, you will have to adjust according to the portions needed and your taste.

CHICKEN STEW WITH DUMPLINGS

This complete, healthy dish provides all the necessary nutrients; you can also prepare this recipe in one pot.

Preparation time: 15 min
Cooking time: 10 min

Ingredients:

For the stew:

Dried or canned chicken

Spices

Flour or cornstarch

Canned or dried vegetables

For the dumplings:

1 pinch of salt

1 cup of flour

2 tablespoons of fat or butter

Water or broth

Procedure:

Start by preparing the chicken stew as in the recipe previously just seen. Meanwhile, prepare the dumplings by mixing all the ingredients and forming a moist dough that is not too soft.

When the stew is hot and almost ready, break the dough into the broth to get all the dumplings the same size of about 1-2 centimeters so they can cook optimally. The dumplings will be cooked when they rise to the surface.

BASIC TORTILLA

Tortillas are a straightforward preparation that can be highly versatile to accompany many dishes. It can be eaten as an accompaniment or create complete dishes with toppings. In this recipe, I will give you the necessary ingredients and the procedure to prepare essential tortillas, and then later, I will show you how to prepare complete dishes with them.

Serves: 3

Preparation time: 15 min

Cooking time: 5 min

Ingredients:

1 cup of flour

Salt (to taste)

2 tablespoons of oil or fat of your choice

Water

Procedure:

Begin by combining the dry ingredients and the oil (or fat of your choice), then add water a little at a time until the dough is soft but not sticky. Continue kneading for about 5 minutes, then let it rest for about 15 minutes.

Next, after the dough has rested, roll out the tortillas not too thick, deciding on the size according to your taste. Finally, cook them over medium heat in a lightly greased skillet, turning them to cook on both sides.

Tortillas can be prepared either on an induction griddle or a heat source such as a wood fire or a gas camping stove; either way, the timing for cooking may change.

TORTILLA WITH RICE AND BEANS

In this recipe, we are going to prepare one of the many complete meals that can be cooked with tortillas. One of the most common dishes is precise with rice and beans.

Serves: 4-5

Preparation time: 15 min

Cooking time: 20 min

Ingredients:

<u>For the tortillas:</u>

1 cup of flour

Salt (to taste)

2 tablespoons of olive oil or fat

Water

<u>For the filling:</u>

1/2 lb of rice

1 or 2 cans of beans

Spices of your choice

Olive oil

Procedure:

To prepare the tortillas, go back to the previous recipe. In the meantime, take care of the rice; once cooked in plenty of salted water, drain it and season it lightly with oil.

On the other hand, drain the beans and combine them with the rice, adding some spices to your liking. If you prefer, you can puree the beans in tomato sauce to make them more flavorful.

Fill your tortillas with the rice and bean filling, then roll them up, forming tasty burritos!

BREAD

Here we come to a staple food in the diet of many people. Bread is straightforward to prepare, costs very little, and versatile. In fact, with bread, you can prepare many recipes or consume it as an accompaniment.

This item is a must in case of survival, as it has a high carbohydrate intake, which gives you sufficient energy. In an emergency, bread can be baked in a Dutch oven, solar oven, wood stove, or on a hearth. You will only need to adjust the temperature and be careful when baking.

Preparation time: 15 min

Cooking time: 25 min

Ingredients:

3 1/4 cups of Flour

2 teaspoons of salt

1 1/2 cups of Water

2 teaspoons of instant yeast

Procedure:

First, combine all the dry ingredients in a large bowl, add the cold water a little at a time, and start mixing until you run out of water. Knead with your hands until the mixture is firm and does not stick too much to your hands. The second step is to cover the dough and let it rest at room temperature.

Within 2-3 hours, its volume will double. Next, lightly dust some flour on a baking sheet (nonstick if possible), divide the dough in two, and give it an elongated shape with your hands. Cover and let the loaves rest for another 45 minutes.

Next, use a knife to make 3 cuts on the buns' surface, bake them in the preheated oven at 474°F and bake for 20-25 minutes until cooked through.

STUFFED BREAD WITH MEAT AND CHEESE

This is a slightly tastier version of plain bread. It consists of making bread stuffed with meat and cheese, which you can replace with other ingredients with whatever you prefer.

Serves: 4

Preparation time: 50 min

Cooking time: 25-30 min

Ingredients:

3 1/4 cups of Flour

2 teaspoons of salt

1 1/2 cups of Water

2 teaspoons of instant yeast

Pieced meat

Cheese

Procedure:

Proceed with preparing the plain bread by taking the previous recipe. Later, when your dough is ready and you have let it rise for the first time, you can now proceed with the filling.

You decide whether you prefer to divide the dough into two large loaves or smaller loaves; this depends solely on your taste.

After you have decided how many pieces to divide your dough into, roll it out, insert the filling in the center, and then you will need to close it into a "pocket."

Let it rise for another 30-60 minutes, and then you can finally bake it. Baking will have to be done in a 350°F oven, while the timing, in this case, depends on the size of your loaves. When they are ready, you can remove them from the oven.

Tip:

You can also make a sweet stuffed loaf; replace the filling with fruit jam, peanut butter, or whatever you like best.

HOME-MADE PIZZA

Pizza is food known and eaten all over the world. It can be prepared even in an SHTF situation since you will most likely find everything you need in your pantry. The most significant benefit it can give you is to boost your morale a lot since it tastes great and appeals to everyone, besides providing you with a high number of calories.

Serves: 4

Preparation time: 1h

Cooking time: 10 min

Ingredients:

4 cups of flour

½ teaspoon of salt

2 cups of water

2 teaspoons baking powder

2 teaspoons of sugar

Olive oil

Pizza sauce/canned tomato

Mozzarella cheese

Procedure:

First, combine all the dry ingredients in a large bowl and then create a hole in the center; add a little olive oil and then the water a little at a time until you get the right consistency (you may not need all of it). Knead well with your hands until you get a soft dough, and finally, let it rise for a few hours until it doubles in volume.

Next, roll out the dough, give it a round shape and start topping it with tomato sauce, mozzarella cheese, and a drizzle of olive oil. Next, you can bake it in your oven/stove or your preferred baking method. The cooking time depends on how you will cook it.

You can season your pizza with as many ingredients as you like. That's the beauty of pizza!

CORNMEAL MUSH

Advantages:
High in carbohydrates, which provide lots of energy necessary for survival.

Serves: 3
Preparation time: 5 min
Cooking time: 5-10 min

Ingredients:

17oz of water

1/2 teaspoon salt

2 tablespoons cornmeal

Procedure:
Boil the water and then add the salt. Now slowly add the cornmeal and stir until all the lumps disappear. Cook for about 30 minutes or until done.

HARD BREAD (HARDTACK)

This preparation creates a hardtack bread that is excellent to keep for a long time, can be used either to break into soups or stews or can be accompanied with fruit jam.

Preparation time: 5 min

Cooking time: 30 min

Ingredients:

1 cup of water

5 cups of flour

Procedure:

Combine the water with the flour a little at a time until you have a stiff dough, at which point, continue kneading with your hands until the dough is smooth. On a lightly floured surface, roll out the dough (if possible, with a rolling pin) about half an inch thick.

The next step is to divide the dough into squares about 3 inches long. Then poke holes in the squares with a fork or toothpick, so the dough bakes well.

The last step is to cook the squares at 375°F for about 30 minutes per side. Once it cools completely, you can package it. If the goal is to store it for a long time, it is necessary that the dough is well cooked and that there is no moisture inside.

HOMEMADE TORTILLAS

Serves: 2

Preparation time: 5 min

Cooking time: 10 min

Ingredients:

1/2 cup of water

1/2 cup of instant corn masa flour

Procedure:

Place all the instant flour and salt in a bowl and create a hole in the center with your hands. Add the water a little at a time, and meanwhile, start mixing with your hands until all the water is used up.

Knead well, then divide the dough into 2 and roll it out. Cut small pieces of dough and start frying them; if you cannot fry them, use an oven.

SPAGHETTI WITH MEAT SAUCE

Serves: 4

Preparation time: 10 min

Cooking time: 20 min

Ingredients:

1 lb of spaghetti

1 can of meat sauce

Water

Procedure:

Bring the water to a boil in a covered pot; once it starts to boil, add a little salt to flavor the pasta, let the salt dissolve for a few seconds, and then add the whole spaghetti (without breaking it up).

Stir the spaghetti occasionally; after about 10 minutes, the spaghetti will be cooked and can be drained from the water. Once drained, add the spaghetti and sauce to the meat sauce. Mix everything well and make sure the spaghetti and sauce are both hot. Serve the spaghetti with meat sauce.

MACARONI AND CHEESE

Serves: 4

Preparation time: 5 min

Cooking time: 15 min

Ingredients:

Water

1 lb of macaroni

Cheese sauce

Procedure:

Place water in a pot and bring it to a boil. As soon as it starts to boil, add salt to flavor the pasta. Allow the salt to dissolve in the water for a few seconds, and then later place the macaroni in the water.

Cook for about 10 minutes until cooked; remember to stir occasionally. Once the pasta is cooked, drain it from the water, add the cheese sauce, and mix well. Serve the macaroni and cheese.

SPAGHETTI WITH TUNA SAUCE

Serves: 4

Preparation time: 10 min

Cooking time: 20 min

Ingredients:

1 lb of spaghetti

3 cans of tuna

1 can of tomato sauce

1 teaspoon of onion powder or chopped onion

Water

Olive oil or fat

Procedure:

First, bring the water to a boil; meanwhile, brown the onion (powdered or fresh) in a pan with olive oil.

Then add the tomato sauce and cans of tuna. Let the sauce cook for at least 10 to 15 minutes, stirring occasionally. Once the water comes to a boil, add a little salt and add the spaghetti as well.

Cook for about 10 minutes until cooked through, stirring occasionally. When the pasta is ready, drain it from the water and add it to the pan with the previously prepared tuna sauce. Stir well and serve.

RICE WOK WITH SPAM AND VEGETABLES

Serves: 4

Preparation time: 10 min

Cooking time: 15 min

Ingredients:

1 can of spam

1 can of vegetables/ frozen/ fresh vegetables

Olive oil or fat

1 and 1/2 cup of rice

Water

Procedure:

First, bring the water to a boil, salt the water with salt, and add the rice. Cook the rice for about 10 minutes, stirring occasionally. Meanwhile, heat a frying pan or, if you prefer, a wok pan with some olive oil or fat of your choice.

Break up the canned spam and add it to the skillet. Let it brown for a few minutes and then add the canned vegetables; if you have the option of using frozen or fresh vegetables, it is even better.

Cook the whole thing for a few minutes. When the rice is ready, drain it from the water and add it to the pan. Mix everything well and serve.

SEAFOOD WOK WITH VEGETABLES AND SOY SAUCE

Serves: 4

Preparation time: 10

Cooking time: 15 min

Ingredients:

1 can of vegetables/ frozen/ fresh vegetables

1 can of canned fish (the one you prefer)

Soy sauce (optional)

Olive oil or fat

1 and 1/2 cup of rice

Water

Procedure:

First, bring the water to a boil, season the water with salt and add the rice. Cook the rice for about 10 minutes, stirring occasionally. While the rice is cooking, pour some olive oil into the pan and brown the vegetables with the fish, seasoning them well with soy sauce.

Once they are well flavored, and the rice is cooked, you can add them to the pan and sauté them for a few minutes. It is now ready to serve.

RICE AND PEAS

Serves: 4

Preparation time: 10 min

Cooking time: 15 min

Ingredients:

14 oz of Rice

1 can of Peas

Chopped onion (or powdered)

Olive oil or butter

Black pepper (optional)

Water or vegetable broth

Procedure:

Fry the chopped onion with some olive oil or butter according to your preference. Next, add the rice and toast it for a few minutes. Now it is time to add the canned peas.

Next, add the broth, which you can prepare by adding some cube powder. Add a little broth at a time and wait for it to be absorbed before adding more broth.

Cook for about 15 to 20 minutes or until the rice is cooked. Before serving, turn off the heat and cream the risotto with butter.

RICE WITH TOMATOES AND CHICKPEAS WITH CURRY FLAVOR

Serves: 2

Preparation time: 10 min

Cooking time: 40 min

Ingredients:

7 oz of cooked rice

200g of canned tomatoes

200g of canned chickpeas

2 tbsp of olive oil

1 sliced onion (or powdered onion)

Spices to taste

Curry

Procedure:

Heat the olive oil in a saucepan and sauté the sliced onion until it softens well. Next, add the spices you like best and stir. Now add the can of chickpeas to the pan and cook for a few minutes, then pour in the can of tomatoes as well and stir everything together.

Add a pinch of salt to flavor everything well. Cook for at least 15 minutes or until everything is well blended. In the meantime, that the seasoning cooks, you will mix the already cooked rice with the curry powder, adjust it according to your taste and then pour the rice into the dishes to make the base.

Now that the seasoning in the pan is ready, directly pour the chickpea and tomato sauce over the curry rice.

TUNA PASTA BAKED

Serves: 4

Preparation time: 15 min

Cooking time: 15 min

Ingredients:

17 oz of Penne

5 oz of cubed mozzarella cheese

4 cans of Tuna

Olive oil

bread crumbs

Chopped parsley

Procedure:

First, put a pot on the stove already salted and bring it to a boil. Then cook the pasta al dente for about 8 minutes, drain it and combine it in an oven dish with the tuna, chopped mozzarella, and chopped parsley.

Mix everything well, and finally, add breadcrumbs to the surface so that baking it in the oven makes it crispy. Finish cooking in the oven for about 10 more minutes or until the breadcrumbs toast.

COUSCOUS WITH TOMATO AND CHICKPEA SOUP

Serves: 3
Preparation Time: 20 min
Cooking time: 40 min

Ingredients:

1.7oz couscous

10.5oz canned tomato (or fresh)

10.5oz canned chickpea

3 tbsp olive oil

17oz hot stock

1/2 onion, finely chopped

1/2 carrot, chopped

Juice lemon

Chopped coriander to serve

Procedure:

First season the couscous with 1 tablespoon oil, a pinch of salt and pepper, then add the hot broth until covered and let it sit until all the liquid is absorbed.

Meanwhile, sauté the chopped onion and carrot in the remaining oil in a frying pan for a few minutes. Next, add the tomatoes (canned or fresh) and chickpeas, and season with a pinch of salt and some spices to your liking. Stir well and cook for about 20 minutes until the sauce is well blended and seasoned. Just before the end of cooking, add the juice of half a lemon.

To finish the recipe, pour the chickpea and tomato sauce on the plate and add the couscous on top; add chopped cilantro and serve.

FRUITY YORKSHIRE PUDDING

Serves: 3

Preparation time: 5 min

Cooking Time: 20 min

Ingredients:

1.2oz caster sugar

3.5oz pack Yorkshire pudding batter mix

Icing sugar to dust (optional)

17.5oz canned fruit in juice, drained

1oz dried fruit

Procedure:

First, heat the oven in static or fan mode to 392°F. Then pour canned fruit and dried fruit into a suitably sized baking dish.

Follow the directions for the mixture written on the package, and then add the granulated sugar.

Add the mixture to the baking dish with the fruit, mix everything well, and bake in the oven for about 20 minutes until cooked through and well browned on the surface. Serve warm or cold, topping with confectioners' sugar.

HOMEMADE TOMATO AND BASIL SOUP

Serves: 3

Preparation time: 5-10 min

Cooking time: 15 min

Ingredients:

1 tbsp of olive oil

1 clove of garlic, minced

28oz of canned cherry tomatoes

3-4 sun-dried tomatoes, chopped

3.5oz of basil pesto

1 teaspoon of sugar

12oz vegetable broth

Basil leaves for serving

3oz sour cream (optional)

Procedure:

First, sauté the olive oil in a skillet with the minced garlic, sauté it well and then add the chopped sun-dried tomatoes, canned tomatoes, the teaspoon of sugar, and the vegetable broth.

Cook for at least 15 minutes until the soup becomes thicker. Then turn off the heat and blend everything with an immersion blender.

Add half portion of the sour cream inside and continue mixing. Next, serve the soup in bowls, and add the pesto on top and the remaining sour cream.

Finish with basil leaves to make the dish prettier to look at.

RED BEAN AND CHILI SOUP

Serves: 2

Preparation time: 5 min

Cooking time: 20 min

Ingredients:

1 can of canned beans

1 can of canned tomatoes (or fresh tomatoes)

2 tbsp of olive oil

Onion powdered (or fresh, chopped)

Herbs

Chilies (fresh or powdered)

Spices to taste

Water or broth

Procedure:

First, sauté the onion with some olive oil for a few minutes in a pot, then add the chili and herbs and wilt those for a few moments.

Now it is time to add the canned beans and the tomatoes. Also, add the broth or water and bring to a boil.

Add the right amount of salt and the spices you prefer.

Cook for at least 15-20 minutes until it is well seasoned and becomes the desired density.

BEAN AND STRING CHEESE OMELETTE

Serves: 3

Preparation time: 10 min

Cooking time: 15 min

Ingredients:

1 can of canned beans

9 eggs

9 slices of cheese

3 tbsp of olive oil

Spices (to taste)

Chives (fresh or dried)

1-2 cloves of garlic, minced

Procedure:

Chop the garlic cloves and fry them for a few minutes in a pan with olive oil, then add the canned beans drained from their water and toast them with the chives and spices of your choice.

After roasting the beans for a few minutes, add the beaten eggs with salt and pepper.

Stir the eggs with the beans, cover the pan with a lid and lower the heat to low. Wait until the top of the omelet is also cooked, and then turn the omelet over with the help of the lid.

Add the cheese slices to the top and cook the omelette for a few minutes on this side. Once cooked, divide the omelette and enjoy.

RECYCLING SOUP WITH PASTA, MEAT, AND VEGETABLES

The beauty of this recipe is that there are no fixed ingredients, but it remains a great complete meal as it will bring you the right amount of carbohydrates, fat, and protein. The concept is simple, create the recipe with what you have at home.

Serves: /

Preparation time: 10 min

Cooking Time: 35 min

Ingredients:

Canned meat (whatever it is)

Tomatoes (canned or fresh)

Pasta (any kind of pasta will do)

Water or broth (vegetable or animal)

Canned vegetables, fresh or frozen

Onion (fresh or powdered)

Olive oil

As for portions, you have to see for yourself based on how many meals you want to prepare; I recommend staying on the 3oz of pasta per person.

Procedure:

The first step is to sauté the onion with some olive oil for a few minutes; when the onion is wilted, add the vegetables, and then, after a few minutes, the meat. Brown it well and then add the tomatoes and finally the broth.

Let everything mix well and bring to a boil before adding the pasta. The pasta should only be put in when the soup is almost ready, as in only 10 minutes, the pasta will be cooked, and it will be time to serve.

SPAGHETTI WITH RED SHRIMP SAUCE

Serves: 3

Preparation time: 15 min

Cooking time: 20 min

Ingredients:

1 can of canned tomatoes

6oz of shrimp (frozen or canned)

11oz of spaghetti

3 tbsp of olive oil

1 handful of parsley

1 clove of garlic

A half glass of white wine

Procedure:

Thaw and clean the shrimp (if they are canned, skip this step), then cook the shrimp with olive oil and a clove of garlic. When the shrimp are nicely browned, deglaze with white wine.

Wait a few minutes for the alcoholic part of the wine to evaporate, then add the tomatoes along with the shrimp. Cook the sauce with the shrimp for at least 10 to 15 minutes to take on the right flavor.

Meanwhile, put the water on the stove and bring it to a boil, salt it and add the spaghetti. After about 10 minutes, the spaghetti will be ready, so drain and add to the red shrimp sauce, add the handful of parsley and mix well.

Now you can serve and enjoy this excellent shrimp spaghetti dish.

SUMMER TUNA SALAD

Serves: 3

Preparation time: 10 min

Cooking Time: /

Ingredients:

2 cans of chickpea

3 cans of tuna in oil or plain

2 cans of green beans (or fresh beans)

2 cans of corn

A few fresh tomatoes (if available)

5 tbsp of olive oil

Juice of 1/2 lemon

Garlic powder

Sesame seeds

Procedure:

Open all the canned foods and drain them, except for the tuna we will use to dress the big salad.

Take a large bowl and start pouring in the chickpeas, green beans, corn, and tuna. Then add the fresh-cut tomatoes, lemon juice, garlic powder, olive oil, and salt. Mix well so that all the ingredients blend well.

Plate the summer salad on the plates and add a half handful of sesame seeds on top to further flavor and decorate the dish.

You can accompany this salad with nachos or bread.

LENTIL SOUP WITH SAUSAGE

Serves: 2

Preparation time: 10 min

Cooking Time: 30

Ingredients:

1 can of lentils

2 sausages (frozen, dried, canned)

1 onion (fresh or powdered)

1 celery stalk

1 carrot

1 can of tomato

Broth or water

Olive oil

1 glass of white or red wine

Procedure:

Pour a little oil into a pot and brown the onion, celery, and carrot, all cut into 4. Cook for a few minutes until wilted; add the sausage, cut it into pieces, let it brown for a few minutes, and then deglaze with white or red wine.

Next, add the lentils and tomato and dilute with a bit of stock.

Season well with salt and pepper and let it cook for about 30 minutes or until it is adequately ready both in texture and taste.

It is possible to accompany the soup with bread or croutons.

VEGETABLE SOUP WITH PASTA

In this recipe, you can use the ingredients you most prefer and have at home, especially regarding vegetables; there is no rule; you can use as many vegetables as you want.

Serves: 2

Preparation time: 10 min

Cooking Time: 35 min

Ingredients:

2 onions

2 carrots

2 celery stalks

2 zucchinis

2 potatoes

Some canned tomatoes

7oz of pasta of your choice

Procedure:

First, wash all the vegetables and cut them into cubes of the same size.

Next, put all the vegetables in a pot filled with water, adjusting the water proportions to the vegetables well.

Salt the water, cover, and bring to a boil. Cook for at least 20 to 25 minutes to season the whole thing. When it looks well cooked, add the pasta you prefer to the soup and cook it for about 10 minutes.

Once cooked, plate the vegetable soup with the pasta.

CREAMY CURRY POTATO SOUP

Serves: 2

Preparation time: 5 min

Cooking time: 30 min

Ingredients:

6-8 medium potatoes

1/2 onion, chopped

1 carrot

Hot water or broth

Curry powder

4 tbsp of olive oil

Procedure:

First, peel the potatoes and cut them into equal-sized cubes. Then add the olive oil and chopped onion to a pot, turn on the heat and sauté for a few minutes.

When the onion is ready, add the diced potatoes and cook for a few minutes.

Next, a little at a time, you will need to add the broth and let the potatoes simmer. Each time the broth dries up, more should be added until the potatoes are fully cooked.

To finish, curry powder should be added and blended with an immersion blender (if possible, otherwise, a manual vegetable masher is fine too).

ZUCCHINI VELOUTÉ WITH CRISPY BACON

Serves: 2

Preparation time: 5 min

Cooking Time: 25 min

Ingredients:

6-8 medium zucchini

1/2 onion, chopped

Hot broth

4 tbsp of olive oil

6 slices of bacon (or something similar you have at home)

Procedure:

Wash the zucchini and cut them into equal-sized pieces. Then add the olive oil and chopped onion to a pot, turn on the heat and sauté for a few minutes.

When the onion is done, add the chopped zucchini as well. Brown well and then begin slowly, adding broth a little at a time until the zucchini is well cooked.

Once they are cooked, adjust the salt and blend everything with an immersion blender.

In the meantime, a few minutes before serving, brown the bacon slices and add them to the dish to create an excellent velouté with explosive flavor thanks to the bacon.

CREAM OF PUMPKIN SOUP AND CHEESE SHAVINGS

Serves: 2

Preparation time: 10 min

Cooking Time: 30 min

Ingredients:

1/4 pumpkin

1/2 onion, chopped

Hot broth or water

4 tbsp of olive oil

Cheese shavings of your choice (parmesan, pecorino, etc.)

Procedure:

The first step is cleaning the squash from the outer skin and cutting it into small cubes, so they cook first.

Brown the chopped onion in a pot with olive oil, and then add the chopped pumpkin. Cook for a few minutes, and then slowly cook by adding broth until the squash is fully cooked.

Once the squash is fully cooked, blend it with an immersion blender. Plate the pumpkin velouté and add a few slivers of cheese at your leisure and a drizzle of olive oil.

VELVETY BEAN SOUP AND BREAD CROUTONS

Serves: 2

Preparation time: 5 min

Cooking Time: 15 min

Ingredients:

2 cans of canned beans

1/2 onion

1 carrot

1 celery stalk

Hot broth or water

Bread croutons

4 tbsp of olive oil

Procedure:

First, chop up the onion, celery, and carrot and sauté them with olive oil in a pot. Next, drain the beans from their water and add them to the pot.

Cook for a few minutes, and then add the broth a little at a time. Continue to simmer for about 15 minutes, adding more broth when needed, until well cooked and blended.

Then blend everything with an immersion blender and serve the bean soup with the bread croutons and a drizzle of olive oil.

BAKED CRISPY BEAN BALLS

Serves: 2

Preparation time: 15 min

Cooking Time: 15 min

Ingredients:

1 can of canned beans

1 egg

Breadcrumbs

1 tbsp of olive oil

Chopped parsley

Spices to taste

Corn-flakes

Procedure:

Open the can of beans and drain them from their water, rinse them under running water and let them drain for a few minutes.

Then move the beans to a large bowl and mash them, helping yourself with a fork or your hands; at this point, add the egg, olive oil, salt, parsley, the spices you most prefer, and the breadcrumbs; adjusting it according to the consistency of the dough.

Once the dough is ready, make patties and then roll them in chopped corn flakes. Fill the pan and bake them in the oven at 356°F for about 15 minutes.

You can accompany these meatballs with a sauce or a side of vegetables.

STUFFED AND STRINGY POTATO CROQUETTES

Serves: 2

Preparation time: 50 min

Cooking time: 15 min

Ingredients:

8-10 medium potatoes

2 eggs (optional)

Breadcrumbs

Chopped parsley

Black pepper

Spices to taste

Cheddar cheese (optional)

Cooked ham

Procedure:

The first step is washing the potatoes and boiling them in plenty of salted water. Cook them until they are fully cooked; they should be soft with a fork in the center.

Once cooked, drain them from the water, peel them and mash them with a fork or potato masher in a large bowl. Add the eggs, bread crumbs, parsley, pepper, spices, and chopped cooked ham.

Mix everything and season with breadcrumbs until the dough is the right consistency; that is, it should not stick to your hands. Work the dough with your hands, shape it into elongated croquettes, put cheddar in the center, and close it with your hands.

Dip it in egg or milk and then again in breadcrumbs to coat. Bake in a 356°F oven for about 15 minutes. Once cooked, enjoy the ham and cheddar-filled potato croquettes.

RICE BALLS STUFFED WITH MEAT SAUCE AND PEAS

Serves: 3

Preparation time: 40 min

Cooking Time: 15 min

Ingredients:

11oz of rice

Canned meat sauce or homemade by you

Canned or fresh boiled peas

2 eggs

Breadcrumbs for breading

Oil for frying (optional)

Procedure:

First, put plenty of salted water on the stove and bring it to a boil. As soon as the water boils, pour in the rice and cook it for about 12 minutes, turning occasionally. Drain the rice and let it cool.

If you have the peas and meat sauce prepared, fine; otherwise, you can prepare them while the rice is cooking.

Once the rice has cooled, add the drained peas (not too many) and mix. Next, using your hands, make rather large meatballs, filling the center with the meat sauce (be careful not to use a sauce that is too liquid).

Close the meatballs tightly by crushing them with your hands, and dip them in beaten eggs and breadcrumbs. Finally, for cooking, you can decide whether to fry them or bake them in the oven.

For baking, 356°F for about 15 minutes, depending on the size of the meatballs. Enjoy!

RICE CROQUETTES WITH HAM, ZUCCHINI, AND CHEDDAR CHEESE

Serves: 2
Preparation time: 40 min
Cooking time: 15 min

Ingredients:

8oz of rice

Boiled ham (or other cold cuts to taste)

Cheddar (or other stringy cheese)

2 Zucchini

Breadcrumbs

1 or 2 eggs

Oil for frying (optional)

Procedure:

First, put plenty of salted water on the stove and bring it to a boil. As soon as the water boils, pour in the rice and cook it for about 12 minutes, turning occasionally. Drain the rice and allow it to cool.

Meanwhile, cut the zucchini into cubes and cook them in a pan or in water. Next, mix the zucchini, diced ham, and rice.

Now you can start forming the croquettes: with your hands, take the dough and create long croquettes, put cheddar in the center and close them tightly.

Dip them in egg and then in breadcrumbs. Finally, for baking, you can decide whether to fry or bake them in the oven.

For baking, 356°F for about 15 minutes, depending on the size of the meatballs. Enjoy!

BAKED VEGETARIAN MEATBALLS

Serves: 3

Preparation time: 15 min

Cooking time: 10-15 min

Ingredients:

Canned mixed vegetables or fresh vegetables if you have them

1 egg

Breadcrumbs

Spices to taste

Procedure:

First, if the vegetables are fresh, cut them into cubes and cook them, or chop them and make them very thin.

On the other hand, if you use canned vegetables, drain them from the vegetable water, cut them into pieces, and put them in an ample bowl. Add vegetables, the egg, a pinch of salt, pepper, breadcrumbs, and any spices you like.

Mix the dough and give it the right consistency; it should not stick to your hands when you handle it.

Following form into patties of the same size. To cook them you can choose how you prefer: pan-fried, fried, baked or steamed.

Whichever way, they will turn out delicious. You can accompany the meatballs with a sauce. Enjoy.

TUNA CROQUETTES

Serves: 2

Preparation time: 40 min

Cooking time: 15 min

Ingredients:

2 cans of tuna

2oz of bread (hard is fine, too)

1 glass of milk or water

1 egg

1 tsp of capers (optional)

Chopped parsley

Breadcrumbs

Oil for frying (optional)

Procedure:

Open cans of tuna and place them in a large bowl. Soak the broken bread with milk or water if you do not have it. Once softened, squeeze the bread well and add it to the tuna; also add the egg, capers, the parsley, breadcrumbs, and some spices if you like.

Mix everything; you need a soft dough that does not stick to your fingers, so if needed, adjust it with more breadcrumbs or more milk/water.

Proceed with forming the meatballs, tossing them again in the breadcrumbs to make them crispier.

Once they are done, you can fry them in oil, bake them in a skillet, or bake them in the oven at 356°F for about 10-15 minutes.

SPAGHETTI MEATBALLS

Serves: 2

Preparation time: 30 min

Cooking time: 20 min

Ingredients:

For meatballs:

3.5oz of minced meat (fresh or frozen)

1 egg

Chopped parsley

Breadcrumbs

Grated parmesan cheese

Salt

For pasta:

7oz of spaghetti

Tomato sauce

Some chopped onion

Olive oil

Procedure:

Place ground meat in a bowl, mix with all ingredients, form into patties, and set aside. Meanwhile, sauté some chopped onion with olive oil.

Then add the tomato and let it cook for 10 minutes, then insert the meatballs and cook them in the tomato. Put the pot with plenty of salted water on the stove and bring it to a boil.

Add the spaghetti and cook for about 10 minutes, stirring occasionally. When the pasta is cooked, drain it and add it to the pot with the sauce and meatballs. Mix everything well, and then serve.

PASTA WITH GARLIC, OIL, AND CHILI PEPPER

Serves: 3

Preparation time: 2 min

Cooking Time: 20 min

Ingredients:

4oz of spaghetti (or whatever pasta you prefer)

Fresh garlic (alternatively, powdered)

Olive oil

Fresh chili pepper (alternatively, powdered)

Procedure:

Place a pot with plenty of salted water on the stove, cover, and bring to a boil.

Meanwhile, in a frying pan, add oil, chili pepper, and garlic (chopped or whole, as you prefer) sauté on low heat for a few minutes until the garlic becomes well browned, with a little cooking water.

Once the water boils, add the pasta and cook for about 10 minutes. When the pasta is ready, drain it and place it in the pan with the sauce.

Stir well to let everything season, and then serve.

PASTA WITH GENOVESE PESTO SAUCE

Serves: 3

Preparation time: 5 min

Cooking Time: 20 min

Ingredients:

4oz of pasta (your choice)

Genovese pesto sauce

Grated parmesan cheese (optional)

To make the home-made pesto sauce:

Basil leaves

Olive oil

Pine nuts

Grated parmesan cheese

Garlic

Procedure:

If you are using ready-made pesto sauce, skip this step; put all the ingredients for the pesto in a blender and blend everything, adjust according to the amounts you have, and adjust according to how you prefer the taste.

Once ready, put the pot on the stove with plenty of salted water and bring to a boil. Once the water boils, add the pasta and cook for about 10 minutes.

Drain the pasta and add it to the pesto sauce, either made by you or ready-made; mix well and serve with a handful of grated Parmesan cheese on the plate.

POTATO PIE WITH ZUCCHINI

Serves: 3

Preparation time: 30 min

Cooking time: 20 min

Ingredients:

4lb of boiled potatoes

5 zucchinis

3 eggs

Bacon (optional)

String cheese (optional)

Parmesan cheese

½ glass of milk

Olive oil

Breadcrumbs

Salt

Black pepper

Procedure:

First, boil the potatoes in plenty of salted water, once cooked drain them and mash them with a potato masher or fork. Meanwhile, cut the zucchini and cook them in a pan or boil them. Next, put the potatoes in a large bowl and add all the ingredients and mix well until smooth and well blended.

Place all the mixture in a baking dish using baking paper or by greasing the baking dish well. Now, bake potato cake in the oven at 356°F for about 15-20 minutes until the surface turns nice and golden. Enjoy!

Tip:

You can make potato cake in so many versions; you can substitute some ingredients and prepare it as you like.

RUSTIC BAKED POTATOES

Serves: 3

Preparation time: 10 min

Cooking time: 15 min

Ingredients:

6 potatoes

Olive oil

Spices

Salt

Garlic

Procedure:

First, wash the potatoes thoroughly under running water. Then dry them and place them on a cutting board.

Be very careful to make many thin cuts close together without reaching the base of the potato, so a kind of accordion should remain intact without reductions.

Proceed with the cuts on all the potatoes, and then season them with oil, garlic, salt, and any spices you like. Let them season for 5 minutes, and then bake them in the oven for about 15-20 minutes at 356°F.

Once the potatoes are cooked, enjoy them while still hot and super crispy.

COLD POTATO SALAD

Serves: 3

Preparation time: 10 min

Cooking Time: 25 min

Ingredients:

6-8 potatoes

Olive oil

Chopped parsley

Chopped garlic/onion

Salt

Fresh chopped tomatoes (optional)

Procedure:

First, wash the potatoes and boil them in plenty of salted water.

When the potatoes are cooked, drain them, let them cool and peel them. Once the potatoes are peeled, cut them into cubes and place them in a large bowl.

Season the potatoes with all the ingredients and mix well to add flavor. Serve and enjoy the cold potato salad.

CHICKPEA VELOUTÉ WITH ROSEMARY

Serves: 3

Preparation time: 5 min

Cooking Time: 15-20 min

Ingredients:

2 cans of chickpeas

1 carrot

1/2 chopped onion

A few sprigs of rosemary (in alternative, powdered)

3 tbsp of olive oil

Broth or hot water

Procedure:

First, open the cans of chickpeas and rinse them under running water, then chop the carrot and onion.

Sauté the onion, carrot, and rosemary in a pot with olive oil for a few minutes. Then add the chickpeas and brown those as well.

Next, add a ladle of broth from time to time and continue like this for about 15 minutes. Once the chickpeas are ready, blend everything with an immersion blender.

CHICKPEA AND TUNA SALAD

Serves: 2

Preparation time: 15 min

Cooking Time: /

Ingredients:

2 cans of chickpeas

2 cans of tuna

1/2 sliced onion

4 tbsp of olive oil

1 handful of olives

Fresh or dried tomatoes

Black pepper

Procedure:

The first step is to open the canned chickpeas, rinse them under running water, and then place them in a large bowl.

Wash the tomatoes, cut them up and add them to the bowl with the chickpeas. Also, add the sliced onion, tuna, olives, olive oil, pepper, and finally salt.

Mix all the ingredients to add flavor and serve.

This salad is perfect for serving with crackers, bread, breadsticks, or anything similar.

COLD SUMMER PASTA

Serves: 3

Preparation time: 10 min

Cooking Time: 15-20 min

Ingredients:

9oz of pasta (fusilli, penne, or other pasta)

2 cans of tuna

Fresh or dried tomatoes

1/2 sliced onion

Parmesan cheese flakes (optional)

Mozzarella cheese (optional)

2 handfuls of olives

Basil or arugula leaves (optional)

4-5 tbsp of olive oil

Procedure:

First, put plenty of salted water on the stove and bring it to a boil. When it boils, add the pasta and cook it for about 10 minutes or until fully cooked. While the pasta is cooking, prepare all the ingredients:

Wash and chop the tomatoes, slice the onion, cut the mozzarella into pieces, flake the Parmesan cheese and open the cans of tuna. Place all the dressing in a large bowl.

When the pasta is ready, drain it and let it cool for a few moments under cold running water. Then next, add it to the bowl with the other ingredients; now add the basil or arugula leaves, olive oil, and olives and mix everything; serve.

Tip:

You can also prepare the cold summer pasta and let it season in the refrigerator for a few hours.

CONCLUSION

First, let me thank you for purchasing my book on survival.

Perhaps you already knew some survival or prepping practices from blogs or other books.

However, you decided to take my book over the hundreds for sale on the Internet. You can't even imagine my gratitude.

Just because you learned the importance of preparation for a more peaceful life marks a first step toward the survivor's winning mindset.

By the end of the book, you may be wondering who I am and what my values are.

Now it is time for introductions:

I am a prepper, educator, and wildlife expert with a degree in physics behind me.

With years of wilderness and urban survival study behind me, I have combined my vast knowledge with my personal prepping experience. With my books, I try to help the modern family prepare for any potential disaster in a friendly and accessible way.

My passion for the outdoors has led me to live a largely nomadic life, gathering a wealth of skills that fuel my work as a survivor.

No journey is ever truly over, and I continue to push toward greater self-reliance and independence every day.

Today, I spend most of my time at home with my wife Sofia and my three children in Houston, United States. With my background as a survivor and Sofia's background as a nutritionist, we are confident that our family could thrive in the face of any disaster.

In my spare time, I snowboard and play amateur tennis. I also go on long hikes with my family, the driving force behind my firm belief in preparing for the unthinkable.

The U.S. Department of Health and Human Services website provides information about natural disasters and public health emergencies.

EMERGENCIES

911 is the universal emergency number.

You can dial it toll-free from any phone.

The 911 operators will alert emergency responders - police, fire department, and ambulance - if needed.

Remember: you must call 911; you cannot text to report an emergency.

Other important Phone Numbers include:

Emergency (Police/Fire/Ambulance): **911**

Local phone directory assistance: **411**

Traffic/Construction on Highways: **511**

ESSENTIAL ITEMS CHECKLIST

You should include in emergency supplies:

- Flashlights or lanterns. You should always have battery-powered flashlights or lanterns with extra batteries available. As a precaution, never use candles during biochemical emergencies. Some biological and chemical agents can be highly flammable.

- Baby wipes. Baby wipes are perfect for keeping things clean when you don't have access to clean or running water.

- Toiletries. You should have a supply of toiletries to keep you clean for at least a month. This includes toilet paper, feminine products, shampoo, soap, shaving cream, and toothpaste.

- Diapers and baby items. You should always have a supply of diapers and formula on hand.

- Children's supplies. Pillows, blankets, and clothes.

- Pet products. If you are sheltering your pet, don't forget his or her needs: food and water, medicine, first aid kit, flea and tick treatments, litter box, newspapers, garbage bags, toys, and treats.

- Toolbox. Simple tools such as a hammer, some screwdrivers, nails, screws, pliers, and a wrench should be in your kit.

- Buckets, bottles, and containers. You can use them to store food, water, and waste.

- Board games and family entertainment. Children can be restless, and this will be an inconvenience. Make sure you have board games or other fun activities to keep your children busy and occupied.

These are the essentials for staying indoors during biological and chemical disasters.

Here is a final checklist you can use to put together your emergency supplies. It includes all the advice in this part, plus additional supplies to help you fully prepare to shut down during a biological, chemical, or medical disaster.

Adhesive tape

Scissors

Plastic sheets (polyethylene sheets, alternative: plastic garbage bags, plastic shower curtain sheets)

Soap

Alcohol-based hand sanitizer

Toilet paper

Facial tissues

Deodorant

Chlorine bleach and disinfectants.

Honey buckets or garbage bags for human waste

Sodium bicarbonate and/or quicklime.

HEPA filter (central or freestanding)

Water - 3 liters per day per person, minimum supply of 10 days

Food - 10-day supply

Can opener

Eating utensils - plastic knives, forks and spoons, plates, paper cups

Dishwashing detergent

First aid kit

Bandages, cotton swabs, elastic bands, gauze, and medical tapes

Denatured alcohol, peroxide, and witch hazel

Aspirin

Antidiarrheal drugs

Multivitamins

Cough and cold medicines

Prescription drugs

Masks N95

Toilet paper

Deodorant

Disinfectants

Cell phone with external/backup batteries

Transistor radios with batteries

Battery-powered flashlights or lanterns with extra batteries

Baby wipes

Toiletries (feminine products, shampoo, soap, shaving cream, and toothpaste)

Diapers

Artificial milk

Children's favorite pillows, blankets, and clothes

Toolbox

Pet food and water

Pet medication, first aid kit, flea, and tick treatment

Pet beds, newspapers

Toys and treats for pets

Board games and other amusements

Buckets, bottles, and containers

ACKNOWLEDGEMENTS

Review this book

Customer reviews
★★★★★ 5 out of 5
104 global ratings

5 star	▓▓▓▓▓▓▓▓▓▓▓▓▓▓	97%
4 star	▏	3%
3 star		0%
2 star		0%
1 star		0%

How are ratings calculated?

Review this product
Share your thoughts with other customers

[Write a customer review]

Thank you for reading this far! I would be extremely grateful if you would take 1 minute of your time to leave a review on Amazon about my work.

REFERENCES

- https://theprepared.com
- Prepper Supplies & Survival Guide: The Prepping Supplies, Gear & Food You Must Have to Survive by Novato Press
- Prepper's Long-Term Survival Guide Food, Shelter, Security, Off-the-Grid Power and More Life-Saving Strategies for Self-Sufficient Living By Jim Cobb
- Preppers Survival: The Ultimate Preppers Guide to Prepare You for Urban Survival by Arthur Cooper
- https://www.backdoorsurvival.com
- https://blog.feedspot.com/survival_blogs/
  - Off Grid Survival | Wilderness & Urban Survival Skills.
  - The Organic Prepper.
  - The Survival Mom.
  - Ask a Prepper.
  - Primal Survivor.
  - Urban Survival Site.
  - The Prepper Journal.

www.ingramcontent.com/pod-product-compliance
Lightning Source LLC
LaVergne TN
LVHW070215080526
838202LV00067B/6821